Praise for *EnergizeGrowth® Now*

"Effective, timely, balanced—this book captures the critical steps for growing a business the 'right way' and avoiding the usual pitfalls of a poor growth strategy."
　—Stephen R. Covey, author
　　The 7 Habits of Highly Effective People and *The Leader in Me*

"Much like my experience at Apple, you will need to know when it's time to stop acting like a bootstrapper and start operating like a growth company. This book is a great resource to ease the transition. By applying these core principles and time-tested planning guides, you will have changed the world for the better."
　—Guy Kawasaki, author
　　Reality Check and *The Art of the Start,* and cofounder,
　　Alltop.com

"I wish I'd had access to this book's wisdom in the past. It's a well-spring of invaluable marketing ideas and wealth-building strategies business owners and management teams can—and should—use to take their companies where they need to go. There's no obtuse theory or hard-to-understand doublespeak here. Just actionable plans anyone can literally start using tomorrow. That makes Lisa Nirell the growth strategy guru for sustainable businesses."
　—Jeffrey Hollender
　　President and Chief Inspired Protagonist, Seventh Generation

"*EnergizeGrowth® NOW* appears at an ideal time to provide small business owners with their rightful wealth, life balance, and peace of mind through great advice, easily applied. Lisa Nirell's advice is more important than any business plan you now have in place."
　—Alan Weiss, PhD, author
　　Million Dollar Consulting

"*EnergizeGrowth® NOW* is simply a fantastic how-to guide for building a great company. Try the ideas in this book and not only will your business grow, but so will you!"
—Marshall Goldsmith
New York Times and *Wall Street Journal* #1 bestselling author of *What Got You There Won't Get You There* and *Succession: Are You Ready?*

"In *EnergizeGrowth® NOW,* Lisa Nirell has written a smart, concise guide for business leaders looking to navigate growth successfully. The book provides valuable tips on how companies can grow better as well as bigger, and how leaders can create the kind of vibrant culture that's critical now more than ever."
—Ray Davis, CEO
Umpqua Bank, and author, *Leading for Growth*

"Lisa Nirell has captured the essence of what it takes to grow an entrepreneurial venture into a successful, sustainable enterprise."
—Jerry Andres, CEO
JELD-WEN Communities, and Chairman of the Board
Clear Choice Health Plans

"What's uniquely cool about Lisa's book is the way she interweaves values with financial success. Making big bucks without values smells. Having high values go unrewarded ultimately destroys beliefs. She keeps 'em together."
—Gary Sutton, author
The Six Month Fix and *Corporate Canaries*

ENERGIZE
GROWTH®
NOW

ENERGIZE GROWTH®
NOW

The Marketing Guide to a Wealthy Company

LISA NIRELL

John Wiley & Sons, Inc.

Published by John Wiley & Sons, Inc., Hoboken, New Jersey.
Published simultaneously in Canada.

For general information on our other products and services or for technical support, please contact
our Customer Care Department within the United States at (800) 762-2974, outside the United
States at (317) 572-3993 or fax (317) 572-4002.

Wiley publishes in a variety of print and electronic formats and by print-on-demand. Some material
included with standard print versions of this book may not be included in e-books or in print-on-demand.
If this book refers to media such as a CD or DVD that is not included in the version you purchased,
you may download this material at http://booksupport.wiley.com. For more information about
Wiley products, visit www.wiley.com.

Library of Congress Cataloging-in-Publication Data:

Nirell, Lisa, 1961–
  EnergizeGrowth® NOW : the marketing guide to a wealthy
company / Lisa Nirell.
      p. cm.
  Includes bibliographical references and index.
  ISBN 978-0-470-41392-0 (cloth)
  1. Business planning.   2. Branding (Marketing)   3. Business
enterprises—Management.   I. Title.
  HD30.28.N57 2009
  658.8'02—dc22
                                    2009000831

10 9 8 7 6 5 4 3 2 1

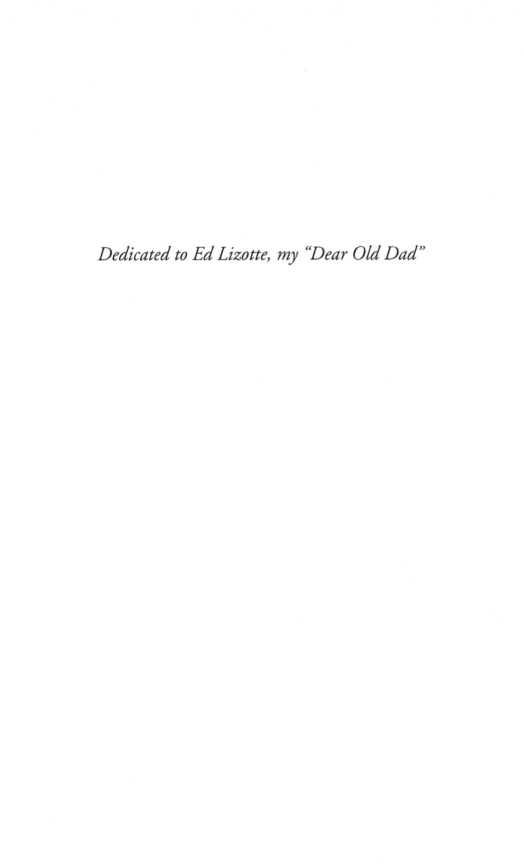

Dedicated to Ed Lizotte, my "Dear Old Dad"

Contents

Will social media increase your company's Wealth Quotient—or destroy it? We take a closer look at social media and its impact on growth companies. Read these tips before you launch your social media plan. We include interviews with companies who have generated six and seven figure sales using LinkedIn, Facebook, and Twitter.

Foreword

Implementation, not ideation, is the essence of entrepreneurship. Thus, the bad news is that soon after the start-up phase, all hell breaks loose. Your initial passion and desire has waned. You have achieved material success, yet you feel empty. You are pulled in multiple directions and are resource constrained—again. Your sales team is struggling to meet demand. Inefficiencies in your business abound. Cash flow is tight—it reminds you of your start-up days. Except this time, you have many more mouths to feed, a real budget to manage, and board members to satisfy.

Whatever happened to the excitement, romance, and glory of the start-up phase when you sat around coming up with ideas? Can you ever rekindle that feeling again?

It's perfectly normal to lose that enthusiasm. When I worked in the Macintosh division of Apple, the shine eventually wore off. Once we achieved great traction and industry accolades, I was ready to move on. That job opportunity was like being paid to go to Disneyland. But don't get me wrong—it was difficult to evangelize a new operating system.

Much like my experience at Apple, you will need to know when it's time to stop acting like a bootstrapper and start operating like a growth company. This book is a great resource to ease the transition.

I met Lisa Nirell during one of my keynote talks in San Diego, California. She then joined my book review team for *The Art of the Start*. Here is what I know about Lisa: She is not some professor who wants to test out the newest 2 × 2 matrix on your dime. She has been selling and marketing high value products and services for nearly three decades. She's a practical, no bull-shiitake, and seasoned marketing evangelist with hundreds of relevant stories to share. Many of them are in this book.

You will benefit from several key principles in this book that business builders face routinely:

- If you have survived the initial start-up phase of your business, it's easy to abdicate positioning and planning to others so that you can keep pursuing new projects (or businesses). Planning cramps your style, right? Don't fall prey to this temptation.

- You can only do so much to position your products and services, so come to grips with the fact that you are not in total control of your positioning. It's okay to position what you offer in a certain way, but ultimately the customers will do it for you. Use the practical positioning tools in this book to get you started, and then see how customers react.

- Now that you're growing rapidly, it's easier to hire a bunch of consultants because you don't think you have the bandwidth to do it all yourself. You'll regret this decision later.

- Nobody can evangelize your company as well as you can. Stay connected to customers, your vision, your pricing model, and your business partners—no matter how busy you are.

- You cannot serve everyone. Don't even try. Avoid distractions and use this field guide to help you focus.

- Finally, Lisa's book reminds us of another effective way to drive your competition crazy: making good by doing good. If you are engaging in activities that do not bring harm to your people or the planet, and you want to make true meaning in the world, you will be increasing your Wealth Quotient or WQ. You'll be doing positive things in the world and ultimately reinforcing your values, your value, and your brand promise.

Use this book to get clear on what wealth and market success really mean to you. Then dive into the 11 planning steps. Validate your information through your customers. Select the right social media strategy. You will save yourself from committing a typical growth company "bozosity"—such as hosting an expensive offsite planning session at the nearest five-star resort.

By applying these core principles and time-tested planning guides, you will have changed the world for the better.

GUY KAWASAKI
Author of *Reality Check* and *The Art of the Start*
and cofounder of Alltop.com.

Plug In

The pursuit of growth at any cost has a price. The demise of companies like Adelphia, Enron, and WorldCom prove that growth has its limits and boundaries. Many firms have ceased to exist due to greed, arrogance, and poor planning. In fact, some small business experts estimate that at least two-thirds of the new businesses you know today will never reach their five-year anniversary.

The past decade has been unforgiving for many business owners. It is not uncommon to know at least one CEO who has simultaneously witnessed a growing bank account and declining health. Much to my surprise, one of my former clients was imprisoned for ethical violations. Another client nearly died from stress and exhaustion at age forty-four. These examples collectively fueled my mission to help business leaders create a positive, lasting impact on the world.

Our desire to make our mark is seldom intentional; it is often accidental. Many of us start businesses because (1) we were laid off from our full-time job, (2) we wanted more freedom and flexibility, (3) we did not agree with our board or supervisor, or (4) we found the trappings of corporate life unfulfilling. We set out to carve our own way with minimal guidance.

For a time, our passion fuels the company's growth. We survive the start-up phase. Then the company takes on a life of its own. Systems, procedures, team politics, drama, and financial pressures compete for our attention. They overshadow our original desire to make a difference. Some of us give in, give up, sell out (well below our potential), or return to the workforce—often out of disappointment.

This doesn't have to happen.

With some thoughtful planning and guidance, you can avoid this situation. In this marketing guidebook, I reveal a contrarian but field-tested approach to planning. I am sharing information that differs from what most of us learned in traditional marketing education programs. You will find many examples sprinkled throughout the book from our clients. They combine the best of both strategic planning and marketing planning into one capsule. As a growth company, you're just too busy to build some detailed plan that will soon be ignored or forgotten. Leave that to the well-established, mature companies with plenty of staff and cash to burn.

The tools and models you are about to learn have taken me seven years to test, improve, and implement. The first 18 years of my career were spent helping companies such as Microsoft, General Foods, Saks Fifth Avenue, IBM, Cisco Systems, JELD-WEN Communities, and Sony. I subsequently conducted proprietary CEO studies in two highly competitive industries: IT services and banking. These experiences helped me identify what worked and what didn't work. They also helped me design approaches that generate the following results for my clients:

- *The quality of their relationships deepens.* Clients invite them into their companies more proactively and give them the time to adequately scope out an opportunity.

- *Their client wallet share—or revenue per client—increases.* Our clients typically raise their fees by at least 10 percent when they work with our team.

- *They abandon the "hours for dollars" billing model.* My clients no longer believe that looking busy and working long hours necessarily translates into building a wealthy business. They begin to feel empowered by the value that they deliver to the market and seek out clients who will reward them for that value. They stop obsessing over revenues and develop more balanced ways to measure success. Clients pay them for the *outcomes* they generate—not for the hours spent delivering the product.

- *Time spent firefighting declines.* The CEO often hires us so that she can start acting like one. She ultimately wants the business to operate without her. We help business owners identify which systems and tools are lacking that will help the company operate more effectively. The CEO can divert her time to more proactive things, such as strategic planning, setting company vision, developing joint ventures, expanding globally, and developing a cohesive, competent executive team.

The stories and guidance in this book will also give you the confidence to implement these systems. They will help your organization rise above the noise of exhaustive, impractical business plans, squandered venture capital investments, and excessive business bravado. I show you how to:

- Understand the benefits and pitfalls of running a growth company.

- Tackle the common beliefs that can sabotage your ideas and distract you from your goals.

- Create a vision of your future that keeps you focused and energized.

- Develop a strategic growth plan that you can actually *use.*

- Adapt more quickly to changes in your market and your business.

- Link your brand to your growth plan to ensure maximum market traction.

- Launch online communities and joint ventures that foster lifelong relationships and customer evangelists.

DISCLAIMER

This book is not about maximizing revenues because getting rich is not every business owner's ultimate dream. For some companies—especially privately held ones—improving our environment, fostering a great culture, maximizing cash flow, or creating more free time may have greater value than the acquisition of more material goods. This book is a how-to guide for any entrepreneur whose dream is to build a highly valuable business that he or she would be proud to sell, exit, or fund. A business he could proudly call his legacy. *A business that reflects the entrepreneur's vision, listens to its customers, and energizes communities.* I hope that describes you.

SOME ASSEMBLY REQUIRED

You play a big role in making this book work for you. The ideas and guidelines require action—plain and simple. Plenty of research books have already convinced you that building a great company is possible, but they fall short of telling you *how to do it*. That's where this book is different. You must be willing to try some of these ideas—in other words, "some assembly is required."

So follow these tips from the owner's manual.

Rule 1: Be Forewarned

If you fear change, this book will confront you. I will ask you to stop doing certain things that no longer serve you or your business. You have to be willing to at least delegate those activities. And—for what may be the first time in your business history—you will be developing a *written* growth plan. But don't worry. I give you plenty of real examples to get your imaginative juices flowing.

One of my top clients averted the development of a business or marketing plan for 20 years—and still grew their organization to $16 million in revenues. Despite their revenue growth, they continually struggled to align their teams around common goals and priorities. The *Energize*Growth® planning process helped them get more focused, improve cash flow, and expand globally.

Some of you will be reluctant to even *begin* constructing such a strategy because you have limiting beliefs about planning (which is covered in Chapter 2). If you take pride in being a do-it-yourselfer, you may not have the patience to gather feedback. That is not uncommon. Follow the planning steps that I have outlined to help you move beyond this apprehension.

Rule 2: Procrastination and Paralysis Are Part of the Journey

As your company approaches a new phase of growth, you may feel like you are in a rut. That is why we dedicate much of Chapter 7 to explaining the common stages of growth you can expect, and what actions you can take when you hit a plateau. If you become familiar with these stages and behaviors, it will be easier to recognize when you hit a brick wall, and it will be much less costly to fix problems. Practicing avoidance behavior (procrastination), and hoping the problem will leave on its own accord, will threaten your company's future potential.

According to a white paper published by Cerius Interim Executive Solutions, ignoring the implications of change—and a common reaction to change such as "analysis/paralysis"—is one of the top five causes of business demise: "Failure to understand the ramifications of a merger or acquisition and failure to account for the business and personnel change management requirements is a key reason the majority (9 out of 10) of M&A activities are deemed unsuccessful. Business transitions that involve restructuring or right-sizing often have unintended consequences that adversely impact the financial well-being of the company" (Cerius Interim Executive Solutions 2008, 4).

Hay Group research also presents a compelling argument for improving your emotional fortitude and resilience. They teamed up with La Sorbonne and tracked the successes and failures of 100 of the largest European mergers and acquisitions. Their survey revealed that more than 90 percent of corporate mergers are deemed a failure because they do not deliver on the original goals that the companies wanted to achieve. They found that the management of intangible assets and the role of leadership are often ignored during the due diligence process. "Intangible assets"—which Ocean Tomo LLC claims comprise a full 73 percent of a company's valuation—include a company's organizational capital (such as organizational structure, agility, and governance), relational capital (such as brand, client intimacy, client loyalty, and internal and external networks), and human capital (such as leadership, engagement, employee productivity, and level of engagement versus compliance). (Hay Group 2007, 5)

I recognize that few growth companies invest the time to recruit seasoned professionals with extensive change management expertise. Yet it is an essential skill to help you successfully navigate the legal, business, financial, integration, and personnel issues that result from growth, mergers, or exits. Even changes that may seem routine—such as a new product direction, corporate strategy, or brand—can prove to be a fiasco if you ignore or downplay the consequences (see Rule 5).

English poet William Blake once said, "Execution is the chariot of genius." Many merger and acquisition experts agree that it is easy to announce a major change such as an acquisition. It is another thing to actually celebrate a successful integration of that acquisition two years later.

Rule 3: You Will Only See Results If You Write Down the Ideas You Want to Implement

People often submit cool new ideas to me. Many of these ideas never see the light of day. Lynne, a participant in a workshop that

I conducted, wanted to share her new company strategy and po-sitioning statement during the session. She prefaced her question with "Here's what I'm thinking about." I stopped her right away, and said, "When you have written down your idea, come back and we'll listen." Lynne's business had taken an entirely new direction. Yet she would not take 15 minutes to record her thoughts. How could anyone in the room—let alone her most trusted peers—ever help her move forward?

Rule 4: Know Your Risk Tolerance

It is easy to ignore the risks associated with the change our growth plans represent. Most of my clients are natural born optimists. What happens if you learn that your team is ill-equipped to bring the plan to life? Or what if you completely forget to interview customers before you launch the plan? Do you have a tendency to think big, set several lofty goals at once, and then lose interest before you ever complete them? Each of these scenarios poses a threat to your plan's success.

I visited a software client several years ago and watched a reckless growth plan unfold. I was hired to help the worldwide leadership team develop an action plan to close more business with their top customers. The pressure was on; they had missed their forecasts for several consecutive quarters. By the end of the session, they were more confident and clear about the steps required to close another $12 million in sales. The overall mood was optimistic and hopeful.

The energy in the room shifted when the CEO arrived.

The CEO announced a comprehensive plan to turn the company around. She then proceeded to present a 36-point turnaround strategy. The strategy was very risky, and was designed for a company with a lot more cash and a much larger resource pool. Furthermore, it distracted them from their number one priority: *growing and retaining their customer base.*

As I watched the color drain from the leadership team's faces, I knew they were really in trouble. They felt overwhelmed. Within one year, this software firm was sold to a European holding company for pennies on the dollar. That 36-point high-flying strategy never left the runway.

Rule 5: Ask the Right People for Help

Request support from leaders who have walked those roads before. Find team members and advisors who can help you apply what you'll learn in this book. Share your concerns and fears with them. Dig deep and express what your inner voice—the risk averse one—is saying. If you are not sure whom to approach, start by designing the profile of the perfect advisory team. They should be able to demonstrate previous success in several areas:

- *They have consistently launched or managed profitable businesses.*

- *They have faced difficult or daunting challenges—and overcame them.*

- *They are willing to be vulnerable.* Nobody wants to be placed on a pedestal. One of the most basic human needs is the need to be accepted, and corporate leaders are no exception. Contrary to urban myth, the number one cause of turnover is *not* salary-related. The same rules apply to the quality of advisors you hire.

- *They are tuned in to what motivates others.* A 2000 study by the Radcliffe Public Policy Center found that over 80 percent of workers in their 20s and 30s placed family friendly work schedules at the top of their priority list. For over 70 percent of workers in their 40s, challenging and rewarding work and good relationships with coworkers were the two most important criteria. The over-50 crowd seek out enjoyable coworker relationships. Guess what ranked sixth for all age groups? *Earning a high salary* (Radcliffe 2002, 2, 3). Before you select your advisors, be sure they understand these important human aspects and "intangible assets."

- *They are willing to stop doing tasks that no longer serve the company,* and they are able to decide quickly what stays and what goes.

- *They tell the truth—no matter what.* The Dalai Lama says: "A true friend is someone who tells you what you don't want to hear." The same could be said for an effective colleague.

- *They can tap into a network at any time and ask for help, referrals, or feedback.*

- *They give credit where credit is due.* Great marketers and planners don't have an unmet need to hog the limelight. Here's an example. *Inc.* magazine recently contacted me for an article on maximizing profits during a recession. I quickly realized that the true champion for the article wasn't me; it was Mark Pollock, the CFO of Avanceon, a client of ours. For the first time in the company's history, they linked their strategic goals directly to their project goals and timelines. Pollock took a very proactive role in that effort. As a result, their collections dropped precipitously from 70 days to 45 days. They were soon featured in *Inc.* magazine for their innovations in managing cash flow during recessionary times. Seeing our client reap the rewards from our work together and the subsequent media coverage were more important than getting my name in the article.

Advisors who possess these skills can help you anticipate what *could* go wrong before it *does* go wrong.

Let me add one more disclaimer: while you read this book, start thinking differently about marketing. Instead of just turning on the marketing faucet when your business needs a boost, make it an integral part of your everyday routine. You must link your marketing to your strategic plan. This expanded view of marketing will energize you, your teams, and your business in the short term, and pave the way for success in the long term.

Accolades and Gratitude

As I child, I often wondered why my mom took so long to prepare her homemade pasta sauce. Now I know. She relied on others to provide the delicious ingredients, including the fresh sausage, basil, mushrooms, and tomatoes. She just couldn't rush the process. She let the sauce simmer for two days to evoke the savory flavors.

Writing this book felt much the same.

I had to wait 25 years to develop the content in this book. I relied on others to review my manuscript and sign permissions. My supporters had to listen to my endless musings about strategic growth and my fears about not having enough information to publish an actual book.

If I have forgotten to mention anyone who contributed to the process, I apologize in advance.

I'll begin by thanking my muse, Henry DeVries. We developed the book title and premise while we sat in Macy's Food court in San Francisco's Union Square. Henry's sense of humor and marketing genius have inspired me for over a decade, and I'm truly grateful.

My colleagues tirelessly reviewed the manuscript. I asked for an hour; they gave me much more. Samantha Hartley, Darrell Crawford, Bob Kreisberg, Bob Phillips, Shawn Solloway, and Collins Hemingway—I salute you!

Over the past decade, several leaders have influenced my point of view on building wealthy, sustainable businesses and strategic growth. My collaborations with Stephen Covey, Guy Kawasaki,

Melissa Giovagnoli, Collins Hemingway, Dan Janal, Susan Lucia Annunzio, Jim Cathcart, Steve Ashton, Alan Weiss, Mark Cavender, Philip Lay, Cathy Hawk, and Carolyn Myss are truly memorable.

My experience with the design and editorial team at Wiley & Sons is unparalleled. Christine Moore provided mentoring and writing inspiration. Jessica Campilango helped me tackle my manuscript design and last minute corrections. Christine Kim brought together a great artistic team and online marketing plan. Matt Holt and Dan Ambrosio gathered all the resources necessary to fulfill the book's promise.

The "nuts and bolts" of delivering the manuscript would not have happened without Holly Joyce. She handled all of the necessary manuscript materials, such as permissions, research correspondence, and citations. As a first time author's assistant, she operated like an old pro.

Inspiration came from many other leaders, authors, and experts. Much to my surprise, my vacation at Hollyhock in British Columbia generated new business connections with people who are truly committed to designing and growing sustainable, healthy communities and businesses. I will be eternally grateful to Joel Solomon of Renewal Partners, Dana Bass Solomon of Hollyhock Institute, David Van Seters of SPUD, Paul Spiegelman of the Beryl Companies, Jerry Andres of JELD-WEN Communities, and Jeffrey Hollender of Seventh Generation. Their pioneering spirit truly gives me hope for the future.

If you ever want to put your partnership to the test, write a book. If you still love each other when it's done, you have accomplished things far more important than the book. My husband Magnus will attest to this. We will soon celebrate our 20-year anniversary. Thank you, Magnus, for being my true companion.

Although Mom and Dad are no longer here to help me "season the sauce," they continue to inspire me through their unconditional love and commitment to my lifelong education. They are sorely missed. Their recipes live on.

CHAPTER 1

Running on Empty

There is nothing permanent except change.

—HERACLITUS

Membership in the growth company club has its privileges. You may have been inducted for a number of reasons. Perhaps you invented a breakthrough product while your competitors were asleep at the wheel. Or maybe you are really adept at expanding a loyal client base. Whatever the reason, it feels good to call the shots and to have completed the start-up phase of your business.

At this stage, it is only natural to wonder what you could ever gain from reading yet another book on marketing and planning. You have already learned all the hard lessons, right?

Maybe not.

Today's current economic turmoil is consuming your energy reserves, no matter how smart, successful, or experienced you are. Stock markets can rise and fall by hundreds of points within just one day. In 2008, "mature" companies such as Washington Mutual and Bear Stearns virtually evaporated overnight. General Motors announced over 5,700 layoffs in the United States and a $2.5 billion quarterly loss. As you will learn later in this chapter, decline happens when you are unaware of the warning signs.

These issues do not just affect mature industries and high-rolling financial firms. It can happen when you are celebrating market dominance and industry accolades. When you have strong (if not dominant) market share, the best people, and the highest potential, you feel unstoppable. You focus on what is working and keep doing it. You struggle to benchmark yourself against your competitors because

you have surpassed them in so many areas. Yet, if you ignore the subtle indicators that your company's continued success is threatened,
you may never muster the energy, resources, or desire to recover from
the decline. Here are some of the most common clues and some ideas
on how to address them:

- *Your ideal client's profile changes significantly.* You notice that
  your current clients begin behaving differently, or your current
  measures of client retention, client satisfaction, and client experiences no longer provide meaningful feedback. Some companies, for example, conduct customer satisfaction surveys by
  polling their salespeople. In these times of fickle clients, basing
  your strategic decisions on secondhand information isn't good
  enough.

- *Your whole product changes.* The term *whole product* is used
  to enumerate all of the deliverables that a customer needs to
  achieve their objectives. In this scenario, you have expanded
  your relationships with partners or other suppliers, and now
  account for a broader slice of the client's budget. For example, you may have recently acquired a training firm to help
  you deliver your offerings. If you have expanded your market
  reach by offering blended learning offerings (such as multime-
  dia programs and online tools), word-of-mouth marketing, or
  online help systems, your impact on your clients' success will
  also expand. These changes in your whole product can significantly affect your company culture, the economic buyers you
  are calling on, the ages of people who want to buy from you,
  your gross profit margin, and your sales cycle.

- *Clients are no longer willing to pay extra for your offerings.* This
  sometimes shows up as declining sales morale and longer sales
  cycles. Now is the time to revisit what makes your product
  or service unique. If great client service and strong client relationships are your only differentiators, it is likely your product
  has become a commodity, or your positioning is stale. With

the pending threat of company decline, you must modify your growth strategy now. Don't wait.

- *Clients are choosing an alternative solution to satisfy the same need.* You are watching your client retention numbers decline, or sales, general, and administrative (SG&A) numbers skyrocket due to a higher cost of sales. If you are losing some of your best clients, quickly determine why the shift is happening. Consider hiring an independent researcher to interview or survey lost clients. Is the alternative solution easier to use, does it take less time, or cost less? Does it appeal to their sense of greed, safety, or ethics? Gather good intelligence.

- *Your margins keep shrinking due to rising costs of doing business.* If the key cost drivers in your business model have outpaced your price increases, it is time to revisit your core offerings and ideal client profile.

- *New, innovative companies are entering your market.* Case in point: the automobile manufacturers once boasted industry dominance in the United States. Over the past decade, the "Big 3"—General Motors, Ford, and Chrysler—have become "the Handicapped 3," while Toyota and Honda have led the charge in innovative hybrid fuel cars. The Big 3 could have adapted, but were wiped out by Toyota's innovation and nimbleness. Now General Motors has reverted to questionable marketing tactics, such as trying to persuade auto buyers to take their Chevrolet Malibu Hybrid seriously even though it boasts a meager improvement of two miles per gallon in city fuel consumption compared to the standard Malibu!

- *You are resisting a new industry shift or technology, even when the market is demanding it.* How often do you find yourself defending your position with your clients? Three years ago, I experienced the perfect illustration of a company's unwillingness to accept an industry shift when I visited a Mercedes dealer. At the time, I was in the market for a new vehicle.

I asked the manager, "What is Mercedes-Benz's strategy for building alternative fuel vehicles?" It was as if I had uttered the unspeakable. The manager firmly replied that they were focusing on fossil fuel technology for many years to come. I quickly chose to buy another brand. Is your company wearing the same blinders?

- *Your key people are married to the way they have always been doing it.* You cannot seem to persuade them to think otherwise. If persistent limiting beliefs define your culture, then selling your business may be a better option than transitioning to a new business model. These limiting beliefs are a surefire way to enter the slippery, painful slope of company decline.

- *The owner has an incomplete or nonexistent succession strategy.* This becomes even more of a threat when the founder faces a health concern, a major life change, a strong desire to pursue a new venture, or apathy. It may be time to measure the percentage of completion of that succession plan—and hold the founder's feet to the fire to stay on track. An outside advisor can help with this process and is downright essential.

- *You believe that growth planning and marketing are reserved for large, mature companies.* How many times do you tell yourself "planning and visioning are important, but I am just too busy to do them?" Maybe you have created a culture of innovation, and planning gets second billing. If this continues to happen, your market dominance is in jeopardy. You are unconsciously passing on this limiting mindset to your team and to your clients. Why would they show any emotional stake in your company's success? You may just be giving them one more good reason to look elsewhere for a job.

- *You are struggling to shift from practitioner mode to leader/ visionary mode.* The habits and skills that helped you attain your first few million dollars typically inhibit your ability to generate the next 10 million. Think about the skilled experts you have met who excel at their trade, and later decided to start their own business in that field. After their first successful growth stage, they are still working in the business. This severely limits their ability to look ahead and divert their time to different activities.

- *You constantly pursue interesting distractions (e.g., new ideas, personal pet projects, or outside ventures).* When you keep announcing new projects and strategies, teams lose direction. They do not see how their jobs tie to your company's success. The information overload can also trigger feelings of overwhelm. Overwhelm translates into paralysis. And paralysis impacts top line growth. By asking some key questions, such as: "What is our core business? Where do we invest? What growth strategy generates the highest return? What is the risk involved with changing direction?" you can get back on track.

- *You continue to sell old, unprofitable products—and still expect your most valuable resources to support them.* Many founders are emotionally attached to their past success and history. This is human nature; we love our babies and don't want them to leave for college. But these blinders prevent us from anticipating new market opportunities, reassigning our top performers to hot new projects, releasing poorly selling/low margin products, or staking a claim in new, highly lucrative markets.

- *You become bored with your current business model.* You have achieved everything you ever dreamed of. Things are running smoothly. The bad news is that innovation has slowed considerably. Your business setting feels more like a family reunion than a high-energy, productive work setting.

- *Your success has become your greatest enemy.* No, this is not a typo. You start breathing your own exhaust. You have crossed that fine line between confidence and arrogance.

If you don't believe this last point can happen, listen to my story.

One glorious sunny day, I flew home to San Diego from London. I was returning from the inaugural planning session with my global account team. Although I was tired from two long days of meetings, I was proud of what we accomplished.

I was the first global account team leader in our company's history to develop a written plan to help us manage and expand the Microsoft account. Our team included some of the best and brightest minds in the global services organization. We were successful because we focused little time on stock price or shareholder issues. Instead, we spent at least half of our time supporting and managing our client relationships.

We set two goals for our two days together: first, develop a written plan that would help us align our account teams across eight countries, and grow the account from $2 million to $11 million within two years. We delivered on what we promised.

Our plan occupied a 4-foot by 6-foot space on the wall. Owners were assigned, initiatives were funded, executive contacts were shared, and travel budgets to Microsoft regional and world headquarters were secured almost indefinitely.

This was the lucrative dream job that I thought I always wanted, and I had reached my personal and financial goals at a young age. My success cup runneth over.

Within three weeks, we scheduled a presentation with Microsoft's key executives in Redmond, Washington. This meeting was essential to gaining their support for our account plan. Our intentions were to announce our broader range of service offerings, and to gain their commitment to the plan we had drafted.

We had invested thousands of dollars just to study their business. We aligned our resources with their highest priority initiatives. As far as I could tell, our planning efforts were flawless.

During my presentation, I shared what we accomplished over the past three years. I discussed how our current programs spanned the globe. I informed the Microsoft executives that we were working on translating our highly acclaimed programs into French, Italian, and Spanish.

Then I presented some disappointing news: Although hundreds of Microsoft employees and partners had attended our programs, we had few business results to show for it. We could only show scant value resulting from their initial $2 million investment.

At that moment, the mood in the room shifted. The senior vice president—our economic buyer—declared, "That is incredible. Why didn't someone bring this issue to my attention sooner?"

Needless to say, we left that meeting without any client commitment to our account plan.

The two-hour flight home from Seattle to San Diego felt like the longest trip of my life. It felt longer than the flight from Heathrow to San Diego!

The reason why we left without a commitment is because *our plan failed to gain the client's commitment to our mutual success.* We had crossed the line from confident to arrogant, and then were stunned when they responded unfavorably.

Microsoft certainly valued our excellent training content—but they had no desire to build a long-term "trusted advisor" relationship with us.

Had I not allowed my own arrogance to cloud my judgment, and focused more on building a trusting relationship, I may have won Microsoft's commitment. For several months, my career ran on empty. I lost confidence. I finally mustered the courage to resign and launched my own successful consulting practice.

I spent the next seven years researching the traits of high-performing growth companies. Now I am clear that planning is useless without the ability to manage your mindset and to engage others in your vision. I have subsequently helped dozens of companies reenergize their teams, their strategies, and their marketing plans.

In the next chapter, you will see the tight connection between planning and mindsets.

Once you recognize the threats to a well-written growth plan with humility and fortitude, you have taken the first step toward building a wealthy company. At that point, anything is possible—including a stress-free flight home from the Seattle-Tacoma Airport.

Energy Booster 1

What market changes and internal limitations pose the biggest threats to our growth plan?

CHAPTER 2

Brains, Beliefs, and Growth Blunders

> The significant problems we face cannot be solved by the same level of thinking that created them.
> —ALBERT EINSTEIN

It is clear that our beliefs can pose one of the biggest threats to our business growth.

It starts with how our minds work.

Humans are a unique breed. We come equipped with some highly sophisticated microchips that are even more intricate than a computer operating system (or a universal television remote control, for that matter). Medical and research communities refer to it as the Reticular Activating System, or RAS, for short.

This part of our brain is believed to be the center of arousal and motivation. According to neurolinguistic programming expert and author Christopher Howard (2004, 27):

> The RAS is responsible for a number of functions, but the one we are interested in is called filtering. This is the process that determines what you become conscious of, what remains in the forefront of your mind, and what simply disappears into the recesses of your unconscious. Whether you know it or not, you tell the RAS what to look for. This is one of the reasons it's important to write down goals.

In other words, your brain contains a microchip that increases the chances of your fulfilling your dreams and implementing your plans.

We are equipped with other types of filters as well, often called *internal filters*. They develop over time and help us formulate our own reality. We are essentially a collection of memories and habits that shape the moment-to-moment flow of the mind.

This book cannot possibly do justice to decades of brain research, nor will it attempt to summarize the countless discoveries within the human potential movement. This would send us *way* outside the realm of the topic of planning and marketing. However, a lack of awareness about the basics of how our brain works ultimately does a serious disservice to one's planning efforts—and further sabotages any chance of success.

Here is a basic synopsis of the human filtering microchip that will help you increase your line of sight and minimize costly planning snafus. As we age, we develop and refine seven filters.

1. VALUES

Our values determine the way we run our lives and how we do things. They are defined as the unique ways of being that guide our decisions, form family bonds, and define our communities. Our values may fall into several categories, such as:

- Health and wellness

- Financial

- How we treat others (community, family, employees, suppliers, etc.)

- Contributions (to community, family, planet, clients, etc.)

- Service (to community, clients, employees, church, etc.)

- Achievement

- Recognition

- Quality (products, work environment, communication style)

- Professionalism

- Fun

- Decision-making style

- Learning environment

- Sustainability

When I work with companies, I have discovered that the most effective organizations invest a significant amount of time establishing their values. When they do this, they find an almost immediate increase in profitability.

This method of doing business was evident when our firm worked with JELD-WEN Communities, a large real estate developer. CEO Jerry Andres approached us because they were facing new pressures to sustain growth. They had launched several key strategic initiatives: three new communities in the Western United States and Mexico, a new brand, and a company-wide reorganization. This was a lot of change for a 400-employee organization to absorb. Teams began experiencing unsteady progress toward their five-year, multimillion dollar "Big Audacious Goal." (BAG). That's when Andres enlisted our help to ensure the leadership team was prepared to face these changes.

By conducting interviews and surveys with their key executives, I identified their leadership strengths, limiting beliefs, and blind spots. I also discovered that they lacked a clear understanding of the company's core values—a situation that was causing some costly project communications breakdowns for new employees and managers.

In addition to completing leadership surveys and consultations, I helped the client refine their core values. Together, we built a strategy to get the entire organization to adopt these values. According to

Andres, "We once had 23 core values which we called our Operating Principles. Now we have 4. Today, the company's key values are responsibility, quality and value, the golden rule, and relationships. Everyone can remember and recite them." These values form the foundation for JELD-WEN Communities success. According to Andres, "To lead a successful company, you've got to be patient and persistent. You also have to articulate as clearly as possible what your vision, mission, and core values are. I used to be a football coach, so I like to tell people I'm still coaching, except the game is different" (Holtzman 2007).

JELD-WEN's experience is not unusual. According to Edgar Schein, a noted organizational development professor at the MIT Sloan School of Management, most other management consultants he has interviewed and studied consider shared values to be critically important for healthy organizational development and sustenance.

Some compelling research further encourages us to take our values seriously. In their seminal book *Corporate Culture and Performance,* Harvard Business School professors John Kotter and James Heskett (1992) surveyed over 200 companies across more than 22 industries for 11 years (beginning in 1990). They found that firms with a strong corporate culture based on a foundation of shared values outperformed the other firms by a huge margin in the following areas:

- Revenue grew more than four times faster.

- The rate of job creation was seven times higher.

- Stock price grew 12 times faster.

- Profit performance was 750 percent higher.

This research emphasizes one of the many reasons why I guide entrepreneurial teams toward reaching consensus on values. Establishing agreement on certain basic, action-oriented, guiding principles regarding how they're going to do business helps an organization create a scalable framework of discipline and decision making.

2. BELIEFS

Beliefs are the second filter that we use to help us determine our own interpretation of the truth. They set boundaries and parameters around the way we think. They can either expand our field of possibility or limit that field significantly. Let's use marketing and planning as a way to frame how beliefs define our business outcomes.

Pete, a successful technology consulting CEO, approached me after one of my workshops in Los Angeles. He told me his vision was to create a $5 million business by 2010. When I asked him how he was progressing toward that vision, he confessed that it wasn't going well. Although revenues were relatively strong, his firm suffered from a "feast or famine" pattern. While his team was completely booked during some months, other months reflected low team utilization. Pete wasn't alone; this is a chronic issue in the consulting profession. After we spent time exploring his business model, we discovered that he had a longstanding belief that marketing was difficult and time-consuming. By identifying and recognizing this limiting belief, we had taken the first step toward eliminating it.

Common Limiting Beliefs

Pete's opinion about marketing is one of many common viewpoints I have heard from hundreds of business owners and CEOs. In fact, several beliefs that sabotage company growth are universal (Middleton, 2008). Here are the most common ones I have heard, and some examples of how they can sabotage your plan:

- *"Planning is difficult, time-consuming, and/or expensive."* One of my clients skated through 20 years of successful growth without ever developing a formal growth plan. What an achievement—or so you may think. Nineteen years into the process, the company experienced a 35 percent annual growth rate and saw its profits plummet. We learned that my client had been over-investing time in the daily operations, and spent little to no time on planning. That's when the CEO called me and decided to abandon this old belief. We helped the company develop a growth plan that every team member can understand and implement. Within nine months, they returned to profitability and have witnessed a significant increase in alignment, commitment, and retention of their top executive team.

- *"Marketing leads to rejection."* This belief wins the Victim Mindset Award (VMA). Behind every innovation is the desire to make the world better, and behind that strong desire is an implicit understanding that risk is involved. And behind risk is the implicit understanding that some plans may fail. How often do you let fear of failure hijack your desires?

- *"It didn't work last time (or, it won't work anyway) . . . so why bother?"* In today's time-starved world, it's easy to filter ideas out quickly and move on to the next new thing. I joined a national trade association last year and had very high expectations about generating new business from my efforts. I became quickly disappointed at the level of decision makers who attended monthly meetings. I then stopped going to meetings and publishing columns for their trade magazine. One year later, I received an inquiry from a fellow member who read my articles and attended one of my keynote sessions. She was ready to do business with me. Within just 30 days, she became a client. If I had abandoned that chance for networking opportunities, this $250,000 client may have never appeared. It leaves me wondering how many other clients I'll never meet!

- *"Marketing is sleazy and pushy."* I can name many examples of sleazy marketing and advertising. One example that comes to mind is the guarantee of reliable Voice over IP phone service from Vonage. When I signed up for their service, I lost between 10 to 20 percent of my calls on any given day. If this belief that "marketing is sleazy and pushy" were really true all the time, every time—then how would companies like Google, Zappos, Apple, Nike, and Coca-Cola continue to build such a strong fortress of brands? The type of marketing that your company does will be based on the importance of the *values* that you have decided on as a whole.

- *"Marketing does not work for this kind of service."* I call this the *arrogance belief.* This one surfaced a few years ago when I spoke to a room full of San Diego business owners. During one of our group exercises, I asked participants to develop an elevator statement—a 20- to 30-second description of what you do, and is used consistently across all of your marketing materials and initial marketing conversations. One CEO, a government contractor, wouldn't participate in the exercise. He firmly responded, "In my industry, elevator statements don't work. The people who *really* need to know what we do—such as army generals—know who we are. We don't need marketing language to help us connect with them." I wonder how his business is doing today, and how that arrogance comes across with his clients.

- *"I cannot launch until I know exactly what to do."* This mindset wins the Perfectionist Mindset Award (PMA). This belief once afflicted one of my clients who consults to the beauty industry. She postponed launching her web site for more than a year. When she attended major industry events, she was ashamed that she didn't have any marketing material to follow up on leads. She was never quite ready to launch that site. Then, after she and I had some blunt discussions about how successfully her beliefs were holding her back, she reframed her mindset and launched the site within 90 days. Her revenues literally tripled 12 months later.

- *"I don't have the right certifications to move forward."* For some professions, education can be the biggest impediment to moving forward. For example, a seasoned corporate attorney in

San Francisco contacted me a few years ago. She held several advanced degrees and had practiced corporate law for 20 years. She was just downright tired of practicing law and desperately wanted a new career in executive coaching. After several attempts to leave the law profession, she approached me for ideas. When I asked her what was stopping her from making the transition, she said, "I can't make a move until I get my executive coaching certification . . . which one do you recommend?" She took more than two years to finally pursue coaching. Her beliefs regarding overpreparation created years of unnecessary angst and frustration. If you are in a profession that requires certification (such as teaching, law, or medicine), then get the best credentials you can. If you aren't, then move forward and pursue what brings you joy.

- *"Marketing is a bother to people."* Let's get this straight before you read any further. Everything you do, wear, or communicate is a reflection of your marketing (or lack thereof). Marketing is essential to your company's longevity—plain and simple. If you believe that you are bothering people, your target market will feel the same way—and they will continue to show resistance to what you have to offer. If you allow this belief to persist, you may never enjoy marketing or sharing your gifts. Your company's full potential will never be realized. That is just tragic.

- *"I am not a marketer—I am a (fill in the blanks)."* How many times have you met the principal in a professional services business who says, "I'm an attorney by trade. I can't make time to do planning. I need to bill more hours. I'll just hire a marketing expert to help our firm with this." This isn't delegation; it's abdication. You are giving up the right to shape and mold the future of your firm. Your brand identity is suspended in time while someone else does the work for you. This is a recipe for failure.

- *"I can do this by myself."* This is a sneaky limiting belief. On the surface, it sounds like a sign of resourcefulness; but in reality, it keeps your business from reaching its full potential. This belief leads you to think, "Hey, I can do this much better and faster than someone else. This won't take any time." Case in point: one of my clients runs a technology consulting firm and kept running out of time to plan and generate new business. For weeks, he tried convincing me that he had other more pressing functions to address—one of which included bookkeeping. I asked what he charged for a day of consulting. He said his fees started at $2,500 per day. Then I asked him what his part-time bookkeeper cost—$50 per hour. That was a short conversation and a turning point in his business. Today, he has a web designer, a bookkeeper, an assistant, and two salespeople supporting a business that has tripled in revenues within three years.

- *"I rely mainly on word-of-mouth referrals."* This is a belief better known as "field of dreams" planning: if you do good work, clients will line up at your doorstep. Here is where this belief can serve you well: (1) You have no plans of creating a predictable stream of revenues; (2) You don't have any employees; (3) You run a lifestyle business. In other words, you accept projects as they come along, and don't have any systematic way or desire to ultimately retire or exit your business under favorable terms. In all other cases, word-of-mouth simply will not do the trick (section titles adapted from Middleton 2008).

3. ATTITUDES

This is the third type of filter—one that is often shaped by your values and beliefs. Your attitudes find a way to sneak into your mindset and can be difficult to identify. Some attitudes are positive; others are negative. For example, one of our clients used to employ a director who would respond to any new company announcement with the comment, "Here we go again . . . another new idea from the CEO!" This attitude of dread and resignation spread like a cancer in the company. Most of their new initiatives failed or took up to five years to take hold. Thankfully, "Mr. Dread" retired soon after we started working with the CEO. We witnessed an immediate improvement in the level of candid discussion and acceptance around new ideas.

4. MEMORIES

Memories are past experiences that shape your current perceived understanding of reality. Think of memories as your way of rationalizing your beliefs. They often form a fuzzy divide between what happened and what you interpreted that incident to signify. From another angle, it's the process we go through to rationalize what we *think* happened and the meaning we assign to it.

Here is an example of someone whose memory was shaping his current reality: Robin is a former client of mine who provides leadership and performance coaching to Fortune 500 firms and world-class athletes. A few years ago, Robin forged a business partnership with another consulting firm, and things went poorly. The alliance cost him thousands of dollars in lost revenue.

Now, let's fast forward to present time. Robin chose to break free from this severed relationship and rebrand his consulting firm with our help. Part of his marketing plan required him to launch a new web site, and I provided him with three reputable web design firms to contact. For nearly a month, he interviewed these firms. He checked references. He scheduled lengthy consultations. Yet, he could not make a choice. When I asked him what was causing the delay, he responded, "I had a terrible experience with another web design firm in the past. Now I'm afraid to make another bad decision."

Robin's memories of poor alliances were haunting him years after the events had occurred. He interpreted that initial single incident to mean that "all alliances and new business partners were not to be trusted." With the techniques presented in this book, Robin was able to break free from these old memories and forge new alliances with confidence.

5. DECISIONS

When you exhibit a certain attitude about an event in your business, the next logical step is to put a line in the sand and make a decision. There is a reason why the word *decide* has the same Latin roots as *herbicide* and *suicide.* This filter in our brain has a sense of finality and doom. It seals our fate if we allow it to permanently drive our business growth. *Choices,* on the other hand, imply more freedom and expansive ways of thinking.

Ken Olson, former CEO of Digital Equipment Corporation (DEC), made several ill-fated decisions in the 1970s and 1980s. He *decided* to ignore the shift from centralized to personal computing. He allowed DEC's engineering culture to dictate their future, no matter how much their customer preferences were changing. He allowed multiple internal groups to compete to see who would invent a personal computer that the market would buy. All three groups failed. Making *decisions* based on a culture that was successful for 30 years may sound like a great idea—if you live in a time bubble! The market was screaming at DEC to change. DEC ignored them and let the innovators duke it out. Their market share gradually eroded and they were eventually acquired by Compaq Computer.

6. LANGUAGE

Our vocabulary is an incredibly powerful tool. Author and consultant Alan Weiss says that "language controls the discussion, discussion controls the relationship, and relationship controls the business" (Weiss 2007). This is especially true when you are selling knowledge and advisory services. For example, how many times do you say,

"We don't want any clients who don't value what we offer ... we don't want to finance our clients' success by undercharging." By focusing on what we *don't* want—instead of zeroing in on what we *do* want—our brains actually ignore the negative word "don't" and direct our energy toward the things that we're working against. Instead, try to use words that positively describe what you're aiming for: "We want sincerely growth-oriented clients who want to significantly increase their bottom line."

7. META PROGRAMS OR THOUGHT PATTERNS

Meta programs are additional thought patterns and filters that determine how you experience the world. Many of our thought patterns exist to help us perform important functions; meta programs are shaped by how you answer these questions:

- *Motivation filter:* Do you typically design growth plans that move you *toward* your vision, or *away from* what you do *not* want?

- *Orientation filter:* Are you typically motivated to do things that others expect you to do (also known as your "should do" list), or are you driven to make choices based on what you do well and passionately?

- *Focus filter:* Do your plans and conversations focus on yourself or on other people? If you lead a professional services firm, do you naturally focus on others when they ask questions or on yourself? Instead of operating in listening mode, too many businesspeople operate in one of two modes: talking or waiting to talk.

- *Success indicator filter:* What tells you that your plan is successful: your own internal monitor, external feedback and validation, or a combination of the two?

- *Decision-making filter:* What form of input do you need to choose a course of action: visible evidence, auditory evidence, written evidence, or experiential evidence (actually doing it yourself)? What kind of information do you usually require to make a decision about a new initiative?

- *Convincer filter:* To what level do you go before you take action? Are you able to decide automatically, or do you need to consider it a few times and review several alternatives? Do you need a certain time period to pass? Or, do you need to be consistently convinced?

- *Leadership filter:* Which of the four methods of leading do you lean toward: leading yourself only, leading yourself and others equally well, leading yourself but struggling to lead others, or leading others and being clueless about guiding yourself on what to do?

- *Energy direction filter:* Do you take action immediately, conduct a detailed analysis before you take action, combine the two, or take no action at all? If you chose the latter, you may be afflicted with "analysis/paralysis."

- *Performance filter:* How do you enjoy performing: independently, on a team, or when you are leading others?

- *Work satisfaction filter:* Which do you enjoy working with the most: things, systems, or people?

- *Preferred interest filter:* What do you love spending your time doing: working with other people, savoring the places you go or live, or collecting things and experiences along the way?

- *Abstract/specific filter:* When you focus on your business or personal goals, do you focus on the big picture and abstract ideas, or do you immediately target specific numbers and measurable results?

- *Comparison filter:* Is your natural tendency to look for similarities in people, places, situations, and things? Do you look for sameness? If so, you prefer routines. If you look for differences, you crave diversity and variety.

- *Challenge response filter:* What is your natural response to situations that arise? Do you let your *feelings* and *emotions* run your life, or are you more objective and thinking in your approach?

- *Time awareness filter:* What approach to time do you take? Do you map out your goals and timelines and consistently show up on time (*through time filter*), or do you live in the moment (*in time filter*)?

Now, take this filtering concept one step further. Let's say that you write a perfect business or marketing plan, but you have a series of old filters that undermine the spirit of your plan. What will happen next? Today's complex, external events can fuel these preexisting filters: The economy. Gas prices. Credit crisis. Childhood obesity. Health care. Education. Tribal wars. Terrorism. These are significant problems that can distract us from the important issues in our lives, and they make choosing more difficult. That's why becoming aware of *how* you approach planning is so critical.

STEPS TO MASTERING YOUR MINDSET

By following these guidelines, you can master your growth mindset and minimize the amount of time you spend on unproductive activity.

Step 1. Acknowledge the Tight Connection between Your Planning Efforts and Your Values

Many people think planning, marketing, and values are separate functions. That's not true. They are, in fact, closely linked. Values are at the heart of marketing. Think of what values you express through every aspect of marketing and planning. The following exemplify the values that our team embraces.

Tell the Truth, No Matter What

Many people embellish information in their plans. Furthermore, they think marketing is a scapegoat for stretching the truth. Effective marketing plans are supported by facts and data, not gut feel. They are supported by programs that educate the target market and provide real value. I feel so strongly about this value that I publish it in every client proposal.

Vision Driven, Yet Focused

Many firms market themselves in a haphazard, unfocused way. Successful marketing plans require real intentional behavior. They entail a need to ask questions like: What do I want to produce and why? What is my plan? What are my obstacles and how will I overcome them? When we help clients implement their plans, the vision statement serves as the anchor. (You will learn more about this in Chapter 6.) This level of clarity of intention and focus can produce extraordinary results.

Make Order Out of Chaos

Our company has developed an uncanny ability to listen to the client's issues and challenges, eliminate distractions, and perform "business triage." Our team constantly asks, "What can we do to simplify this business or marketing plan by removing any extraneous, unnecessary steps?

Dedication to Measurable Results

Unlike many advisory firms, my group only works with clients who are willing to take actions that drive significant, measurable results.

We do not offer any off-the-shelf training events or canned solutions. We invest whatever time is required to make the client win and empower them to become self-sufficient in our methodologies. Our planning systems and tools are designed with this in mind.

Healthy Balance

An energized growth plan creates healthy conditions for growth in your company. Your clients and employees are inspired by it; it allows them to clearly see how their roles tie directly to your most important priorities and goals. Confusion and resignation are minimized. As I mentioned in Chapter 1, wealthy companies no longer imply "growth at any cost." The sign of a great leader is one who creates time to reflect. Remember: We are human beings, not human *doings*. We love working with clients who consistently find ways to recharge their batteries. Whenever our clients reach a significant milestone in their plan, we encourage them to nourish themselves with vacations, retreats, celebrations, and other restorative practices. In turn, they inspire employees to do the same. The plan is therefore viewed as a gateway to freedom, not an obligation.

By linking your values with your marketing philosophy, you can begin to embrace marketing planning as a crucial element in your business,—not simply something you practice when business is slow or when an economic downturn hits.

Step 2. Recognize When You Are Facing a Fork in the Road, or a Choice Point

While knowledge, skill, education, and intelligence are key elements to a company's success, *decisiveness* during times in transition may just be what you need to propel you forward.

Carol S. Dweck, PhD, is one of the world's leading researchers in the field of motivation and has identified two basic types of mindsets in her book, *Mindsets: The New Psychology of Success.* She refers to them as either *fixed* or *growth* mindsets. People with a *fixed mindset* (those who believe their intelligence is fixed) prefer to take on projects that will make them look good. They are generally image-driven and are afraid of looking bad. This prevents them from doing things that can stretch them and help them increase their competency—even when they might badly need those new skills (Dweck 2006).

Four years ago, I consulted with Joe, a regional manager for a Fortune 1000 company. Joe was a master of his profession. Within 10 years of working in the industry, he owned a $2.5 million home in a private San Diego community. But after 18 years, Joe was tired of the mortgage industry. He had a passion for buying and restoring old homes and selling them at a handsome profit. That's when his real mindset emerged.

Even though Joe had plenty of financial reserves, education, and family support, he was stuck in a stagnant mindset. The thought of relinquishing his $15,000 annual country club membership, $95,000 BMW, and $2.5 million home to get what he *really* wanted out of life was too scary. He would not take the leap of faith because it could tarnish his image. Joe still sends me periodic e-mails describing his ongoing struggle to pursue his passion.

People with a *growth mindset* truly believe that learning requires a lifelong commitment. They are highly eager to expand their horizons, even if it means that they may look foolish or make mistakes.

Garry Ridge, CEO of WD-40, models this behavior consistently. He has even coined a term for this mindset—he calls it the "Learning Moment" (www.learningmoment.net). During our interview, I discovered that Garry has turned the company from a single best-selling product model to a profitable collection of nine brands. Garry embraces this concept as one that permeates their corporate culture. Whenever one of his team members makes a mistake, he encourages them to approach him and say, "I just had a 'learning moment.' This is what happened, and here is what I am doing to prevent that from happening again." By encouraging candor and experimentation, Ridge sustains a learning culture that is willing to take risks and model a growth mindset. Not surprisingly, WD-40 celebrated a record year in 2007 with $308 million in sales and a 19 percent return on equity (G. Ridge, personal communication, August 17, 2005).

Step 3. Remind Yourself That You Hold the Power—Not Your Thoughts

Thoughts are energy, and negative mindsets block your energy. If you come across a limiting belief in your company, avoid the temptation to analyze that belief in great detail. Do not discuss *why* marketing is hard, expensive, or won't work. This is a losing battle. Simply sit down with your team and collectively admit to each other: "This is an existing mindset, and it may not be serving us." Then ask these questions:

1. Is it true?

2. Can you absolutely know that it's true?

3. How do you react, what happens, when you believe that thought?

4. Who would you be without the thought?

Then *turn it around* (the concept you are questioning), and don't forget to find three genuine examples of each turnaround. In other words, develop a new mindset that is the opposite of your old mindset (Katie 2008).

Remember—your job is not to deny or suppress the mindset; just acknowledge it exists. Ask yourself if that belief is really true—all the time, every time. Explore how your company functions in the world when that thought is allowed to rule your actions and choices. Then write down what kind of leader you can be without that mindset. You will notice that a new story—a more empowering one—will emerge. To learn more about this powerful process, I recommend that you read Katie's book *Loving What Is*.

Transforming your old beliefs about growth can reenergize your team quickly. If you ignore these mindsets, you are delaying the inevitable: a failed plan. You are also missing the chance to market your gifts and develop talented teams. This is simply a travesty because you prevent your organization from creating enough opportunity to do what they love; and furthermore, you short-change your clients and communities from reaping all the benefits you deliver.

Viktor Frankl—a concentration camp survivor, Nobel Peace Prize nominee, philosopher, and professor—reminds us of our power to choose in *Man's Search for Meaning: An Introduction to Logotherapy:* "everything can be taken from a man but one thing: the last of the human freedoms: to choose one's attitude in any given set of circumstances, to choose one's own way" (Frankl 1963, 104).

Effective planning is about carefully choosing your mindset, honoring your values, and recovering rapidly when you hit a bump in the road. Now you have the preventive medicine and tools to make smarter choices—and build a wealthier company.

Energy Booster 2

What steps can we take *now* to minimize the top limiting beliefs in our company?

CHAPTER 3

Say No to the Good, and Yes to the Great

In science the credit goes to the man who convinces the world, not the man to whom the idea first occurs.
—SIR FRANCIS DRAKE

For years, I have wondered why so many intelligent business people struggle with making their plans come to fruition. Why do so many of them end up gathering dust on the shelf—even when the leadership team is aligned toward a common goal?

It's because most current planning methods reward the wrong things: *good ideas, complexity,* and *busy work.*

Before you can truly energize your business growth, you have to learn how to focus your energy. Start by avoiding traditional ways of planning.

In the traditional business setting, planning starts innocently enough. Some smart executives convene at a gorgeous resort. They sequester themselves for three days for strategic planning. Some facilitator waltzes in with only the best of intentions.

The participants go to their "happy flip-chart place." They agree on goals. Some even hold themselves accountable to reach those goals. They even give them a fancy name: SMART goals (Specific, Measurable, Achievable, Realistic, and Time-bound).

Then the meeting ends and business as usual sets in. People get distracted. Their "crackberries" start buzzing, vibrating, and pulling them in other directions. Various commotions—often shrouded as emergencies and crises—take over.

Hard-working participants soon feel demoralized. As the accountability fades, they wonder why they spent so much time and energy to develop this plan. Resignation and apathy set in. Their well-intended planning exercise becomes a distant memory.

This feeling of futility is not unlike the grief I felt when I visited my father for the last time. When I transferred him from the hospital to hospice, his hands were chilled and his pulse slowed. He told me, "I'm ready to go." Everything leading up to his last rest stop told us this was coming. For the past six months, he had allowed his home to fall into disarray. He lost interest in socializing. He stopped paying his bills. Generally, he lived a pretty unhealthy lifestyle.

Dad had survived two bouts with cancer, a brief boxing career in the Navy, and a tour of duty during World War II, but now he had chosen to stop fighting.

By the time I arrived in Naples, Florida, to give him my last goodbyes, I knew the end was rapidly approaching. He had lost the will and the strength to stay alive. Dad passed away a few days later on May 27, 2008.

In our personal lives, losing a loved one is hard. It takes us time to grieve, heal, and move on. In business, letting go of things that no longer serve us is just as hard, and it requires us to make tough choices.

Much like my personal life, my career has survived its own highs and lows, including two recessions. In the late 1980s and in 2001, I saw hundreds of companies shift from high growth to slow death. Many practiced some rather debilitating habits. One of the most common, life-limiting ailments is something I call "time deficiency syndrome." It's that constant feeling that there is not enough time in the day to complete everything that needs to be done.

The way in which we spend our time has shifted dramatically. In the United States, the average workweek has swelled to 48 hours, surpassing the Japanese. It doesn't just affect our work hours; it's now affecting the way in which we work, travel, and play. YPartnership's National Travel Monitor™, an annual survey of 2,100 leisure travelers in the United States, found that respondents are planning fewer leisure trips in 2008 than in 2007, primarily due to concerns with current economic conditions (YPartnership 2007).

Here are clues that you suffer from time deficiency syndrome:

- *You never feel a sense of completion and accomplishment.* You keep adding more items to your to-do list because you find comfort in looking busy.

- *You live in a constant state of being overwhelmed.* This means you fall victim to your circumstances. You will notice that you allow things to run your life and consume you. Much like the travel survey respondents, CEO's blame their sense of overwhelm on an ethereal being called "the economy." This is just an industry-accepted term for "circumstances."

- *You cling to the familiar.* When time deficiency syndrome overtakes us, we become chronically unwilling to stop doing certain activities. You are unwilling to let go of resources and activities that no longer serve you—even when it's painful, costly, and damaging to your brand. One of my clients once tried to convince me that working on QuickBooks was a better use of her time than prospecting, writing articles, networking, or speaking.

Perhaps you have seen these energy drainers in your own company. They are especially present after you experience a growth spurt. They appear in many forms, such as tolerating poor paying clients, retaining nonperforming employees, and allowing disorganized teams to flourish. They may also be unreliable vendors or stodgy banking relationships. Or, you may have old assets that you keep forgetting to retire. The list goes on.

Case in point: I recently worked with a consulting firm. They have been in business for 18 years and boast a stellar client list. During the economic boom in 2004 to 2006, they enjoyed a huge influx of projects. They grew from 4 to 11 employees. Soon after this happened, they were bleeding cash. They were highly leveraged. Their receivables grew to $90,000 in 2007—and they only had $5,500 in cash. They avoided any cost-cutting actions for more than 9 months. Instead, the founder took a "wait and see" and "work harder" approach. When I asked her what cutbacks she was willing to make, she adamantly refused to lay off employees or cut costs. She was clinging to a business model that had long passed them by—even though it was killing the company.

At some point, the cost of holding on to these costly resources and unprofessional relationships will far exceed the cost and temporary hassle of releasing them.

My client Jacque tempted her company's demise for the past few months—even though her business and client base had doubled. Jacque owns a consulting and recruiting firm that helps beauty business owners increase their profitability by reducing their time to market and increasing employee productivity. Her company's results speak for themselves. Within just one year, she saved one client $2 million. The good news spread fast. Not only did she deliver great results, she began communicating those results more effectively through her web site and networking activities. Clients started flocking to her.

Jacque did not prepare for the onslaught of additional work and administrative burden. Her office became disorganized. Her e-mail volume exploded. She upgraded her online presence and created a brand new web site. Creating time for her family became more and more challenging.

Within just a few weeks, her passion for her work began eroding. As we both discussed the situation, we realized she had only two choices. She could either: (1) ignore the problems and keep moving forward; or (2) slow down, take stock of what was happening, and make adjustments.

Thankfully, Jacque chose option B. Then she got to work.

First, she pulled her 12-month written goals out of the drawer.

For three consecutive days, she logged every daily activity on her schedule, and how much time she was spending on each. It was a long list! In the left column, she ranked each activity on a 1 to 10 scale. This scale reflected which activity most supported her goals (10) and which supported them the least (1). Then she took that list and determined which activities supported her strengths the most and which supported her strengths the least.

Activities that scored low on the strengths or goals scale were dropped entirely. The remaining activities that ranked high on the scales were assigned one of two action steps:

1. *Delegate* the activity to someone who enjoys it, and does it well (if not better than you).

2. *Delay* it; revisit in 1 to 3 months.

Great things began to happen. When Jacque shared her list with her husband, he was fully supportive. In fact, he had not previously realized how overworked she really was. Then she made specific requests to her business colleagues and friends. Everyone offered to help her in the short term while she recruited resources. Her girlfriend agreed to come by once a week and handle housekeeping activities. Within 48 hours, every low scoring activity was handled.

This may sound like a simple task. It is. However, it's not easy to ask for help and say no to nonessential tasks. Most entrepreneurs pride themselves in doing virtually everything themselves. As a result, their business dies a slow death. Often, they are not as fortunate as Jacque to catch it early, when cash flow is still positive.

Even business author and greatness guru Jim Collins (2001) warned us about this business malady in his timeless book, *Good to Great:*

> Most of us lead busy but undisciplined lives. We have ever-expanding "to do" lists, trying to build momentum by doing, doing, doing—and doing more. And it rarely works. Those who built the good-to-great companies, however, made as much use of "stop doing" lists as "to do" lists. They displayed a remarkable discipline to un-plug all sorts of extraneous junk. (p. 139)

Delegating, delaying, and dropping activities and projects are not just good ideas. Think of them as preventive medicine.

One of the most valuable learning points from Collins' book is his description of the "hedgehog concept" (Figure 3.1).

Jim and his research team discovered that the really great companies understand deeply three things about themselves:

1. *They know what they can be best in the world at.* This is very different from identifying your core competence. According to Collins, "you might have a competence but not necessarily have the capacity to be truly the best in the world at that competence. Conversely, there may be activities at which you could become the best in the world, but at which you have no current competence" (Collins 2001, 118–119).

2. *They know what energizes them, and what they are passionate about.* Do you wake up in the morning filled with excitement and gratitude for your clients? Do you have a method for

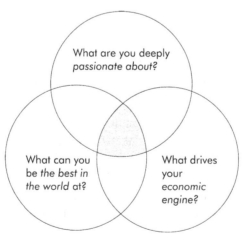

FIGURE 3.1 Hedgehog Concept

Source: Good to Great: Why Some Companies Make the Leap and Others Don't, by Jim Collins, New York: HarperCollins, 2001, p. 96. Copyright © 2001 by Jim Collins. Reprinted with permission from Jim Collins.

conquering the limiting beliefs and thoughts that creep into your day? Or—are you working because you have to?

3. *They know what drives their economic engine.* Often, you can find what drives your economic engine by finding the one denominator that has the single greatest impact on your business. In services firms, these are typical economic drivers that we've seen:

- Net profit per employee,

- Average client engagement size,

- Realization rates (total number of working hours in the year divided by total billable hours per employee),

- Client retention rates, and

- Lifetime value of a client.

Great companies typically take four years to identify their hedgehog concept. This is not an overnight exercise. A wise person once said that it is difficult for us to read the label from inside the bottle. That's why we need to ask our clients and strategic partners for feedback and insight.

Gathering feedback not only helps you identify what to stop doing; it also helps you harvest the most value from your business by focusing more time and energy on what you do best.

CALCULATE THE ROI FROM YOUR HEDGEHOG

Defining a hedgehog—and leveraging it effectively in the marketplace—can be a struggle for many companies. Clients who join our *Energize* Marketing Action Groups remind me of this frequently. Our group members are growth-oriented professionals who want to ultimately sell or exit their business, but find their company is undervalued. In these groups, our participants often have a dozen great marketing ideas. We call it "shiny penny disease."

The disease shows up in myriad ways. The first symptom is a calendar full of random marketing activity. This may include multiple networking activities, numerous blogging projects, Twitter "tweeting," speaking engagements, trade group volunteering, nonprofit work, search engine optimization projects, website redesigns, and so on. The disease spreads quickly and consumes excessive resources. Their natural response is to throw up their hands and say, "This is too much to handle, so I will stop doing them."

When this happens, it is time to remove the emotion from the equation and apply some logic. I invite my client to pause, review and write down their vision and values. Then I ask the following 10 questions that can measure the return on investment (ROI) on activities that support their hedgehog:

1. What measurable goals will help you realize your vision?

2. Which good ideas on the list get you closer to realizing your vision?

3. How will your clients benefit from that strategy?

4. How will management benefit from it?

5. How will this accelerate growth and innovation?

6. What is the financial reward for investors? How will it affect the bottom line?

7. What is the cost of *not* doing it? What is the impact on your investors, management, clients, and growth/innovation engine?

8. What is the total estimated cost of implementing this idea?

9. What is your action plan to implement this idea? The action plan must include answers to the following questions:

- Who owns the action step?

- By when will it be completed?

- What resources are required?

10. What's the total return on investment for this idea? Calculate ROI by using this formula: (Total Benefit divided by Cost to Implement = ROI.)

These 10 questions will help you get clear on what activities fit within your hedgehog. I guarantee you will no longer be consumed by the "good idea machine"—a contraption that will truly suck the life out of a visionary business owner.

What if you already have a good hedgehog, and just want to maintain your current level of growth? You can implement three proactive steps:

1. *Ask your CFO, CPA, or bookkeeper to run an analysis of your most profitable clients and projects.* Then develop a (gulp) strategy to eliminate the bottom 10 percent of your client base. Your bottom 10 percent can be defined as:

    - Clients who refuse to provide you with referrals;

    - Clients whom you believe have initiated or participated in unethical behaviors;

    - Clients whose values are much different than yours;

    - Clients who take more than 30 days to pay—even after repeat requests;

    - Clients who challenge you on every request, suggestion, and recommendation;

    - Clients who constantly haggle on your fees; or

    - Clients who are unwilling to contribute a testimonial or case study.

2. *Invest in a survey that compares your company performance against your competitors.* This will lower the possibility that the hedgehog you invented is a carbon copy of theirs. SageWorks Analyst by ProfitCents is an excellent tool for this analysis.

   Select a tool that has the ability to evaluate several key areas of your business. For example, ProfitCents prompts the consultant to enter data from the company's financial statement into an online form. The system then analyzes the financial data and processes the data through its patented algorithm.

   In less than one minute, the software generates a report in plain English. Using a five-star rating system and clearly organized summaries, this report assesses the company's long-term health through several lenses, including sales, liquidity, profit margins, assets, employees, and rate of borrowing.

   This report will show you where you may be over-investing or under-investing resources. You may also find places where you are lacking resources and focus to attain your annual goals.

   Here's what makes ProfitCents so palatable: the total time required to input your financial metrics is less than one hour. A certified ProfitCents Consultant will require no more than two hours to review the results with you. Appendix B contains an example of a ProfitCents Extreme Report.

3. *Spend the next 90 days validating your hedgehog by gathering external feedback.* Times change. Client attitudes shift. Competitors consolidate and gobble up market share. The hedgehog you proudly used five years ago has an expiration date.

   External feedback will help with this. Bring your top advisors together. Some may be suppliers, business partners, team members, and clients. Request time to interview them by phone and follow the interview protocol that we have included.

This is one sure way to fall out of the "doing" trap. It will give you clues about what your company really does best . . . and where to focus your business development efforts.

Tips for Discovering (or Redesigning) Your Hedgehog

- Whenever possible, hire an independent, objective interviewer to help you collect external feedback. Remember—you're only human, and it's highly likely you will put subtle pressure on others to agree with you (forcing *groupthink* to set in). Alternatively, you may experience *selective recall*—only remembering the facts that reinforce the assumptions you prefer. Or, you may exhibit *confirmation bias*—and seek out only opinions that match yours.

- Develop a cross section of contacts that represent 10 percent of your total client base. This may be 6 business partners and clients; it may be 600. These contacts will fall into one of three categories: clients with whom you have a long track record, clients you recently lost, and some who are almost ready to do business with you. Feel free to include strategic allies and partners in this process. *Be sure all three categories are included and interviewed.*

- Ask your founder or CEO (if that isn't you) to personally call these contacts and request their candid input. *This is really important in setting the tone of the process.* She should ask the interviewee to allocate 30 minutes over the phone. Give them the name of the interviewer and ask them to schedule a call with the interviewer. *Do not*

(continued)

(Continued)

conduct online or fax surveys—you will NOT get the quality of information you need.

- Tell them it is very important feedback to help you discover what you do really well. You value their input on how THEY think you can expand on that. Thank them sincerely for their time.

- Remind them this information is 100 percent confidential, and will not be attributed back to the source.

- Send them a personal handwritten thank you note after the interview.

13 Questions to Discover Your Hedgehog

1. Tell us who you are and what you do. How did you first meet us?

2. *Best experience:* Looking at your entire experience with (*your company name*), remember a time when things went especially well. A time when it seemed that someone went the extra mile to make something happen. Tell me about that experience:

   - Who else was involved?

   - What were they doing?

   - What were you doing?

3. How does this compare to most of your experiences with (*your company*)?

4. What was this situation/problem costing you before you hired (*your company*)?

5. *Business results:* What do you value the most that this company helps you do more effectively? (Listen for their values, goals, and dreams.)

   • Hard-dollar ROI or business results?

   • Soft-dollar ROI? Value of the relationship to you personally?

6. What can you do now that you could not do before? Please provide examples.

7. What's unique about (*your company/service*) that you can't get with other firms?

8. *Core value:* What do you think are the top two to three core values of (*your company*)? In other words, if it did not exist, it would make the company look completely different than it currently is (your interviewer is listening for core beliefs, ways of doing business that are pervasive and easy to identify).

9. There are lots of companies out there selling the hottest, newest (*solution or service*). Did you ever think the (*solution or service*) could be another one of those solutions or that solving your problem just required "more hard work?"

(*continued*)

(Continued)

10. What would make you recommend other companies to hire this company? (Whatever they say, ask, "Why is that important?" so we can really uncover their belief systems and values.)

11. What advice would you give a company that is considering this type of service?

12. As a professional in the (*industry*) business, what do you think is the future of the industry? What changes are we likely to see in the next three to five years? How can a company like (*your company*) be positioned to meet those changes and challenges? (This is a great way to uncover new business opportunities that you may have ignored in the past.)

13. If you had three wishes for your relationship with (*your company name*), what would they be?

These powerful questions will give you solid clues to your strengths, values, and highest return opportunities. Be open to what you hear—and what's next for your company.

Interview Preparation Notes

Ponder this: What external contacts would you speak to?

_____

_____

_____

_____

Lost clients:

_____
_____
_____
_____

Longstanding clients:

_____
_____
_____
_____

Business partners:

_____
_____
_____
_____

Post-Interview Notes

1. What adjectives do your clients use to describe their experience of working with you?

2. What were the most common values your clients see in your company?

3. List the top five measurable outcomes your clients said you deliver:

(*continued*)

(Continued)

    a. _____

    b. _____

    c. _____

    d. _____

    e. _____

4. What makes your services unique?

5. What are the areas that your clients want to see improved?

6. What offerings do your clients value the LEAST from you? How can you delegate, outsource, or stop doing this entirely?

7. What new opportunities do your clients suggest you pursue? What new offerings can you add to your services portfolio?

When you have completed these interviews and summarized your findings, your understanding of your strengths will deepen.

HEDGEHOGS SIMPLIFY SEGMENTATION

Once you have clarified your hedgehog, you will most likely need to rethink your marketing plan. How you define "ideal client" will also tend to change.

If you are like many companies, you currently follow a traditional view of your ideal client. You look at market size, company location, demographics, and the level of the decision maker in the organization. In fact, many firms often pursue the same segment as their competitors. This often leads to "me too" marketing and price competition.

When I began working with Pat, she followed the "traditional" market segmentation approach. Her firm, Tydak Consulting Services, LLC, in Thousand Oaks, California, helps mid-sized companies bridge the gap between business ROI and information technology.

Originally, Pat focused her marketing efforts on small to medium sized businesses in Southern California and Arizona. She experienced her share of unresponsive decision makers and poorly managed companies who seldom implemented her recommendations.

After we began working together, her definition of an ideal client expanded. Today, she only accepts clients who are truly open to working with outside services providers for the long term. They have to be willing to refer her to other clients. Today, nearly 80 percent of Tydak's new clients are generated through referrals. Furthermore, Pat and her team will not work with companies who want a few contractors to help them through a temporary technical or operational challenge.

Regardless of how you define your segment, *the number one purpose of segmenting the market is to establish an addressable set of target clients who share a common problem that you can help to solve differently and better than any of your competitors, and in which you will be rewarded handsomely.* The segment MUST be willing to pay you well for what you offer and to solve a big problem or aspiration. In Chapter 5, we show you a very effective (and somewhat contrarian) method to identify your ideal client.

Segmentation also fuels your confidence to adhere to your "stop doing" list. Internet pioneer and serial entrepreneur Lori Prokop has a memorable way to describe the "stop doing" process: "say NO to the good, and YES to the great."

Lori practices what she preaches. Over the past 20 years, she has launched more businesses than most people will ever work for in their entire careers. Today, Lori is a Google AdWords expert and a results-producing copyrighter. She has been voted by her peers into the International Marketers Hall of Fame. Her book publishing client list includes Ted Turner, Jim Palmer, and Mark Victor Hansen.

Lori represents 50 bestselling authors, coaches, and speakers on a variety of personal growth and success topics through her Keyboard Culture online community (www.keyboardculture.com). Her hedgehog is clear: she is best in the world at launching web-based businesses, gets paid handsomely by her clients for her leading edge marketing services, and is passionate about "advancing messages of Love and Light by helping hundreds of people get their messages of hope out into the world."

Some entrepreneurs may find Prokop's message offensive, ethereal, or too heart-centered. But others will find that it resonates with them immediately. By following one or more of the steps outlined in this chapter, your tribe will find you—just like hers have found her (L. Prokop, www.keyboardculture.com).

Every day, I am reminded that life is a metaphor for business. Our growth plans are living organisms. They require constant care and feeding. When this happens, they have the potential to change the world and leave a positive impact in their wake. We cannot prevent the eventual demise or sale of our business. But we can prolong them. And, with preventative care, we can help it remain vital and strong.

Energy Booster 3

What shiny pennies are distracting us from our growth potential?

CHAPTER 4

Increase Your Wealth Quotient

What's the use of a fine house if you haven't got a
tolerable planet to put it on?
—HENRY DAVID THOREAU (1817–1862)

A few years ago, the CEO of a $50 million technology firm hired me for a keynote speech at his annual company meeting. I always prepare extensively for these in-house sessions by interviewing key executives and employees. These interviews revealed a company that appeared well organized and highly regarded among its peers. They were profitable. Cash flow was strong. They had operations in three major Western cities. So far, so good.

The CEO had inherited the company from his father in the 1970s. He considered himself semi-retired. He had survived a heart attack, and announced that he was scaling back on his work activity. On his seventy-first birthday, he promoted his son to company president.

I originally thought that the CEO was on a clear path to exit the company gracefully. Boy, was I wrong!

At the conclusion of my keynote, I discovered several dysfunctional traits within the company. The CEO held the corporate staff in a tight grip. Nobody made a move without conferring with him, whereas the president—his son—had nothing more than a fancy title. The board consisted of old family friends that the CEO had appointed. His son spent most of his time resolving political battles across their three branch offices. The CEO talked a good game about his succession plans, but he never took any actions to transfer his majority ownership.

As a result, his son felt disempowered, and the employees experienced a company that was stuck on permanent hold.

This was a classic example of a perpetually dysfunctional, adrift company. Regardless of their repute and strong balance sheet, they had a questionable future. Who would ever want to buy this company? Were they truly "wealthy?"

This situation underscores the fact that your business is a living organism—something that will continue to grow and thrive long after you've played your role in it. Keeping this in mind, you must ask yourself: what can you do to ensure that your company creates long-term wealth?

I developed this book to help you plan for these events, and to ensure that you can eventually sell or exit your business on your terms, at a time of your choosing. You were attracted to this book because you prefer not to die at your desk. By focusing on the right actions, you establish the conditions for a rewarding exchange of your life's work for a successful retirement.

This chapter highlights the reasons that some business owners are destined to leave a memorable imprint on the planet, while others are not. It also shows how you can increase the profitability of your business in the years prior to a sale. That may mean 5 years, and it may mean 15; it's never too early to plan your exit.

We will *not,* however, spend time addressing other important wealth-building aspects of growing your business, such as:

- Extensive analysis of various company valuation formulas;

- How to prepare, value, and market your business when the time is right to sell;

- Legal and financial preparation to maximize yield; or

- Wealth preservation tips and strategies.

Myriad business brokers, attorneys, and financial advisors are adept in these areas. They focus heavily on the quantitative aspects of selling your business. As important as those factors are, they only provide a partial definition of wealth.

HOW WE DEFINE WEALTHY COMPANIES

Plato once said that, "The path to wisdom begins with a common set of definitions." You must develop a fundamental understanding of wealth and how it is created before you can determine how wealthy your company truly is. Let's explore the various ways in which wealth has historically been defined and decide which definition best serves your business.

A *Wikipedia* search resulted in this economic definition of wealth:

> In economics and business, wealth of a person or nation is the value of assets owned net of liabilities owed at a point in time. The assets include those that are tangible (land and capital) and financial (money, bonds, etc.). . . . Measurable wealth typically excludes intangible or nonmarketable assets such as human capital and social capital. In economics, "wealth" corresponds to the accounting term "net worth."

The word *wealth* was originally derived from the old English word *weal,* which means well-being. It was a term used to describe someone who possessed great qualities. In most business circles, however, this traditional definition has gotten lost. In today's modern times, online marketing pundits will tell you that wealth is measured by the level of income derived from the passive revenue sources (such as online product sales, affiliate programs, book royalties, and investment dividends) that allow you to live without depending on a job.

In my ongoing search for the most useful definition of wealth, I returned to a tried and true resource—the father of modern management and renowned business thinker Peter Drucker.

Drucker defined the purpose of a business this way: "Any business enterprise has two—and only two—basic functions: marketing and innovation. These are the entrepreneurial functions. Marketing is . . . the unique function of business" (Drucker 2004, 80).

These are certainly two cornerstone requirements to optimizing business value and creating a *wealthy* business over time, but do they provide the whole picture of a wealthy company?

Because I wasn't sure that this definition captured every element of the kind of wealth that I was hoping to define, I kept searching. I thought, "Wouldn't it just be easier if we could look at history's greatest business leaders and model ourselves after them? I can just read Napoleon Hill's *Think and Grow Rich* over and over and emulate the likes of Andrew Carnegie and John Rockefeller—right?" But that approach didn't seem adequate, especially since the examples are outdated and solely represent the older white male population. Times have changed dramatically since the publication of this ground-breaking book, and although some of the basic lessons still apply today, people's perceptions of business, happiness, and fulfillment have shifted significantly.

The current role models and definitions of "wealth" are enough to make your head spin. And let's face it—very few media outlets praise today's *Fortune 500* companies for "possessing admirable qualities." So let's pause for a moment. You're reading this book because you want more out of life than cash in the bank, right? You want to perform work that creates meaning and significance in the world. That's why these definitions no longer serve us. Therefore, *you must define wealth in your own way; in a way that honors your values, your vision, and your core strengths.*

Why Old Definitions Don't Work

Here's why those older definitions may serve as reference points, but don't manage to fully define your business's true potential. Over the past decade, many firms have gone from "hero to zero" at breakneck speed. The primary reason for this may well be that these companies never fully understood the more intricate parameters of wealth. The cases of corporate giants WorldCom, Enron, and Adelphia taught us that strong market share, political power, and money do not necessarily translate into wealthy—or successful—companies. Rising foreclosure rates, spiraling national debt, and resource scarcity have made the unprecedented rise in our prosperity over the past decade a mixed blessing.

This lack of vision and purpose has caused millions of seemingly displaced workers and seasoned executives to ask: "Is all of this hard work worth it? Is *that* all there is?" The real blessing underlying today's corporate talent exodus is the fact that many people are seeking a more meaningful balance between money and happiness, which is causing them to redefine wealth on their own terms.

Global activist and fundraiser Lynne Twist has raised over $150 million in individual contributions for the Hunger Project and has been honored by the United Nations. A few years ago, Twist authored a book titled *The Soul of Money* that inspired me to question some traditional wealth models. *The Soul of Money* explores how people relate to money, and Twist posits that money should be earned and spent in ways that reflect our highest values. While she is all for making money, she firmly believes that the pursuit of money is not an end in itself. Rather, it is a means to acquiring something that is of greater value—value that depends on an individual's perspective.

Twist's point of view runs contrary to what traditional media outlets are telling us, including CNN (a network to which I affectionately refer as "Constantly Negative News"). She asserts that there are enough resources to sustain everyone on earth, but despite the abundance, she claims that too many people are enslaved by "the great lie of scarcity." From her perspective, people perpetuate several toxic myths:

- There's not enough.

- More is better.

- That's just the way it is—*so why bother?* (Twist 2003, 49–53)

Whether you agree with Twist or not, her writing compels us to look at wealth in a different way, and to perhaps challenge our long-accepted notions of this concept. Before you define the meaning of a wealthy company, you need to answer some deeply personal questions:

- *What is your relationship with money?* You may not realize it, but you do indeed have one. You can choose to be empowered, expansive, knowledgeable, fearful, or ignorant. A friend of mine, for example, chose the ignorant path. For the past two years, her training business has barely earned enough income to pay bills. Her relationship with money is: "I don't understand it, and I'm not good with numbers." Until she shifts her mindset to a more empowered, responsible view of money, she will remain trapped in the hand-to-mouth financial paradigm.

- *Do you live an expansive or restricted financial lifestyle?* The answer to this question depends heavily on the type of financial environment in which you were raised. For example, while I was growing up, my parents would issue a subtle warning after every successful job milestone I achieved. Whenever I got a raise or closed a big sale, they would say, "Remember to save your check for a rainy day. You never know when you will need that money." I always worried whether I had enough funds in reserve. When I realized that wealth reflected my state of mind, I shifted my mindset from "Save your money for a rainy day" to "I am so happy and grateful that money comes to me easily and freely from a variety of sources." And guess what—it does!

- *Do you constantly suffer because you still don't have enough?* In other words, when you achieve a milestone, are you still restless and paranoid? The root cause of this conundrum is not business ethics, childhood memories, or corrupt politics. It is an eroding value system that aims to prey on human insecurity by perpetuating the myth that the more things we have, the happier we will be. Marketing is not just about promoting your services to give your clients more tangible business results. It is also about improving their peace of mind, increasing their repute, improving team alignment, reducing error rates, and a host of other intangible benefits.

- *Have you become cynical and resigned around money?* Do you think to yourself—in terms of your financial situation—that "This is how it is, and it cannot improve"? For less mature companies, this can be a real showstopper. I was watching a reality television show last week that highlighted the trials and tribulations of "financial resignation." On Bravo TV, a short-lived show titled "Tabatha Takes Over" showcased a highly sought-after beauty salon owner who helped distressed salon owners turn their business into a financially solvent enterprise. In one episode, the family-owned salon was over $1 million in debt. The husband and wife had refinanced their salon three times by using credit cards and home equity lines of credit. Furthermore, they were actually living on bags of beans and canned tuna fish. They told Tabatha, "It has been this way for over two years, and we don't see a way out of it." They saw no way out of their debt-laden life. Thankfully, Tabatha's wisdom and guidance turned their situation around.

Exploring your relationship with money can help you uncover potential wealth barriers. It will also help you define a more sustainable, longer lasting formula for wealth. By reviewing your results from the hedgehog exercise in Chapter 3, you will gain insights on how you can maximize your contribution to the world.

Major companies are getting on board with newfound notions of wealth and committing resources to the conversations around wealth building. "Spiritual capital" and "Spiritual intelligence" are buzzwords in some of the most conservative corporate boardrooms—including investment firms. Mutual fund pioneer Sir John Templeton was a living example of how to turn financial success into creation of wealth. Templeton spent two decades exploring the nuances of spiritual capital, and he spent his final years dedicating himself to life's bigger questions. He started his illustrious investment career in 1937 and was later touted by *Money Magazine* as "the greatest global stock picker of the century." He established the Templeton Foundation in 1987, and it grew to $1.5 billion in endowments. At the time of his death in July 2008, Templeton had given away close to $70 million in annual grants. Templeton modeled the attributes of creativity, innovation, and intuition—qualities that are cornerstone traits required for wealth building.

Before you begin to worry that this book is taking you into a spiritual dimension, recognize that this expanded wealth mindset can lead to greater self-awareness, a more clearly defined sense of purpose, a lifelong dedication to service and compassion, and a willingness to ask basic questions. Let's look at some ways you can position your company for successful growth and eventual exit.

Most CPAs, attorneys, investment bankers, and business brokers will tell you to focus on some fundamental issues to improve your company valuation. They claim that valuation is the key to maximizing your sales price, and they will refer to these basic topics as "value drivers." According to Ned Minor—a Denver, Colorado, based attorney and author of *Deciding to Sell Your Business:*

Value drivers are those characteristics that influence a buyer's decision about how much to pay for a company. These include:

- A stable, motivated management team;
- Good and improving cash flow;
- Operating systems that improve sustainability of cash flow;
- A solid, diversified customer base;
- Effective financial controls;
- A realistic growth strategy; and
- A facility appearance consistent with asking price. (Minor 2003, 69–70)

While these value drivers are important and sound, they tend to assume that the company's collective mindset is operating at peak performance. Many are not. Creating a wealthy company *first* requires mastery in two areas:

1. Your ability to consistently focus your resources on creating sustainable value (the "outer game" of wealth).

2. Your mindset about money and wealth (the "inner game" of wealth).

These are the foundations that help you assess your Wealth Quotient.

WHAT'S YOUR WEALTH QUOTIENT?

We have developed seven criteria to help you assess your Wealth Quotient—or WQ. Your chances of running a wealthy company worthy of a successful exit increase dramatically by taking some important preliminary steps. These steps will help you grow your company's WQ, and streamline your ability to establish strong value drivers. These are the *new* rules for creating a wealthy company:

1. You consistently and confidently express and demonstrate your value to the market.

2. You are paid handsomely for the value you deliver.

3. You continuously innovate.

4. You focus on business endeavors that educate and inspire other people.

5. Your business endeavors honor and respect the natural environment.

6. You have enough of the right clients—you know who they are; you can explain your ideal client to others very clearly;

and you market to them in an authentic, consistent, and systematic way.

7. You provide your stakeholders, investors, and employees enough time for family, friends, and personal growth.

Let's look at each WQ principle in more detail.

1. You Consistently and Confidently Express and Demonstrate Your Value to the Market

Two years ago, I performed a small experiment. While traveling across the United States speaking to CEO associations and trade groups, I asked participants a simple question: "If you conducted an informal poll in your company, what percentage of your employees would consistently and correctly answer the *What does your company do?* question?" After many of them responded with overly optimistic responses—upwards of 50 percent—I asked another question: *Okay, now what is the REAL answer?* They sheepishly responded: *Less than 10 percent.* How can you expect to consistently predict your company's growth when 90 percent of your employees cannot explain what you do?

Market perception begins with clear communication. It's our responsibility as a company leader to explain how our services deliver measurable results. Every day, it's our job to prove that our offerings are worth substantially more than the fees we charge.

Even today, many business owners think that just because they can produce a quality product or service, their company will command a high price. That is simply not true. Your ability to execute well usually makes the company sellable, but the ability to execute is just the minimum standard for attracting interest in the marketplace. By itself, it is not a significant value enhancer. *You have to communicate a story worth telling.*

2. You Are Paid Handsomely for the Value You Deliver

Volumes of books have been written on this subject. Alan Weiss' *Value Based Fees* provides many practical examples to help you ask for what you are worth, and suggests dozens of ways to command better fees (Weiss 2002). But the real work begins with—you guessed it—your own perception of your firm's services, and what they are worth.

The flow of money also depends on your willingness to receive what is owed to you. This may sound like entitlement, but it isn't. If you have clearly proven the return on investment you deliver to clients, then you have earned the right to command healthy fees for your services.

What I'm about to share will rattle most attorneys, accountants, and architects. Wealthy companies get compensated based on the results they deliver. Struggling companies get compensated based on hours worked. What a trap. Can you add more hours in the day? Certainly not. Can you really get ahead while more and more hourly worker functions are getting outsourced overseas for a fraction of the fee? Never.

Do you ever wonder why the rich get richer, and the poor get poorer? It's simple. If you put a ceiling on your firm's earnings, your WQ will hit a ceiling, too. If you are not training yourself to receive your share, you will see money flow to someone else. Many marginal businesses suffer because their teams do not believe that they have earned the right to be rewarded for their effort. This sets people up to be perpetual victims of economic swings and external events.

3. You Continuously Innovate

Some people shy away from exploring innovation because they incorrectly assume that innovation requires technical wizardry. While technology may be involved in various aspects, innovation is primarily about making your company and employees better for the benefit of your customers and stakeholders. It is aimed at improving your business practices so that you set the standard in your industry.

There are a number of reasons that you *must* innovate. First, your market demands it. Customers vote with their wallets. In today's heavily networked world, pragmatic clients will shop around, read social networking sites and product reviews, and then buy from the source that offers the best value with the least risk.

Second, your competitors require you to stay on your toes. You may know your direct competitors, but what about the indirect form—"alternate uses of capital"? Technology is another, more insidious form of competition. Just stop and think of the products, services, and industries that no longer exist because of an advance in technology: Betamax, AOL, traditional phone service, etc.

Finally, *strategic business buyers require innovation.* Minor defines strategic business buyers as those companies who are looking for assurances about the future viability of any business they acquire—particularly when they're considering paying a premium. They need to see a pattern of how your company has consistently innovated in the past, and how you intend to continuously innovate. This gives them confidence that your company's future is not in jeopardy from direct, indirect, or technological competition.

4. You Focus on Business Endeavors That Educate and Inspire Other People

This principle takes its inspiration from one of the most influential political strategists of our time—the Dalai Lama. He reminds us that interdependency is an essential part of our flat world:

> The need for love lies at the very foundation of human existence. It results from the profound interdependence we all share with one another. ... The more we care for the happiness of others, the greater our own sense of well-being becomes. ... Interdependence, of course, is

a fundamental law of nature. . . . In today's materialistic society, if you have money and power, you seem to have many friends. But they are not friends of yours; they are the friends of your money and power. When you lose your wealth and influence, you will find it very difficult to track these people down. . . . That is the moment when we learn who is really helpful and who is completely useless. So to prepare for that moment, to make genuine friends who will help us when the need arises, we ourselves must cultivate altruism! (Gyatso n.d.)

If you think excellent service will instantly translate into inspiring and compelling potential clients to buy from you—think again. Many banks continued to report staggering losses between 2007 and 2008, and bad lending practices only provide a partial answer. Think of all the homeowners who were approved for subprime loans—even though the lenders *knew* that they demonstrated a history of bad spending habits. *The lenders who approved those loans degraded other people.*

In 2007, we interviewed dozens of community bank CEOs. Our conversations led us to uncover some sobering data. For one thing, very few of the CEOs could truly explain how they inspire and retain clients. Even fewer could describe how they managed to do it differently than their competition. We heard the phrase "great customer service" so many times that we felt as if the bankers were eavesdropping on each others' conversations.

Whether they were working with commercial or retail clients, most bankers never stopped to elicit the emotional reaction their clients express when they select them for their financial needs. Similarly, if your offer is not compelling, people will not pay you enough to earn the gross profit margins that will enhance the marketability of your company.

The most powerful key to discovering what your clients think is to *ask them*. (Revisit the survey questions in Chapter 3 for insights.)

5. Your Business Endeavors Honor and Respect the Natural Environment

My own personal experience at Hollyhock, Canada's largest educational retreat center, gives me hope that more and more of us view our business as a conduit for environmental responsibility. The organization was established over 20 years ago and now runs nearly 100 educational programs annually with just a $3.5 million budget. Their purpose is quite clear: "We exist to inspire, nourish and support people who can make the world a better place." I met with Dana Bass Solomon, president of the institute, and asked her about the links between their reverence for nature and the bottom line. Solomon responded:

> We exist to inspire, nourish and support people who can make the world a better place.
>
> As we enter our twenty-seventh year, we continue to run our business with a "triple bottom line" approach: We exercise our care and concern for the natural world, and our focus is on "social profits," or community outreach. All dollars coming into Hollyhock are reinvested into our work and mission.
>
> Our famous Hollyhock garden is a model for how we do business. We feed and nourish the soil. We plant high quality seeds. We selectively harvest. Some plants are used for compost; others we give away. And we constantly pull weeds. Sometimes, we have to trim back. We tend each part of the garden—the soil, plants, produce, and flowers. And the results are magnificent.

Hollyhock's concern for the environment goes farther than that. In order to reduce their carbon footprint, they host a very popular rideshare board on their web site. The board became so successful that they opened up the program to all local residents of Cortes

Island. They encourage seminarians to travel in groups. On any given day, 100 visitors and guests come and go from the property. Finally, their onsite solar panels now heat 60 percent of the hot water used on the property.

Hollyhock recently converted their retreat center to a not-for-profit organization. Their practices have made an impact on for-profit concerns worldwide (D. Bass Solomon, personal communication, August 13, 2008).

6. You Have Enough of the Right Clients

Who are your clients? Do you really know? Last spring, I wasn't so sure. My firm was overdue for a "branding makeover." I could not easily describe the key things that make *Energize* Growth® unique. I developed a short survey to uncover these qualities within our client base. I soon discovered that our firm has three qualities that, when combined, provided a one-of-a-kind offer to our clients. They include healthy balance, making order out of chaos, and an intense focus on measurable results. These qualities evoke emotional responses from my clients and frame all of my branding activities. This brand clarity helps to establish trust and confidence with our clients.

It also helps us establish early whether we are a good fit for each other. During my initial conversations with prospects, I send them to our web site. Then I ask them to visit several short pages that explain our company values and our ideal clients. Giving your prospects a short reading assignment has several advantages. First, it tells you how serious they are about exploring working with you. Second, they can self-select. If they find that our values are misaligned with their own, the sales cycle will be short and inexpensive for all concerned. They know what to expect when they engage our firm. They get a sense of our team's personality, and how we will treat them over the course of our relationship. Prospects gain comfort in knowing that we have worked with many other clients facing their issues. A potential client is able to see the measurable results that we have helped our other clients generate. They can immediately see that the return on investment far exceeds the money they will spend with our firm, and that we are expecting to be adequately rewarded for our expertise. This clarity protects me from entering into price negotiations.

Educating potential clients about your company's core beliefs and practices are fundamental prerequisites to selling your services at an attractive gross profit margin. According to Michael Sipe, CEO of CrossPointe Capital, "Business buyers want to see gross margins in excess of 40 percent. If you are not able to command a 40–50 percent gross profit margin, the marketability and selling price of your business will suffer greatly" (Sipe 2008, 21–22).

Seventh Generation, a self-proclaimed pioneer among socially responsible companies, is very effective at educating its target market about the benefits of healthy and sustainable living—and their margins reflect that. According to President and Chief Inspired Protagonist Jeffrey Hollender, "It comes down to serving people the way they want to be served. It may involve helping customers with things that have nothing to do with our products, such as finding a holistic health care practitioner." They distribute an educational newsletter to more than 170,000 online subscribers. Their "Ask Science Man" feature on their web site allows customers to post any question to their chemists. The results are impressive. They have averaged more than 30 percent revenue growth and at least 50 percent profit increases for the past five consecutive years (J. Hollender, personal communication, October 6, 2008).

7. You Provide Your Stakeholders, Investors, and Employees Enough Time for Family, Friends, and Personal Growth

There is no shortcut around this principle. The only way to ensure ample time for these important endeavors is to write a practical *Energize*Growth® plan that highlights the most important priorities of the company. Without it, your team will always feel overwhelmed, overworked, and underpaid. We review the components of this plan in greater detail in Chapter 6, but the main purpose of this plan is to design a bright future for your company. As you get closer to selling your company, recognize that strategic buyers will want to purchase a system that they perceive has a high probability of (1) making an ever-increasing *amount* of money for them in the future, or (2) increasing their market leverage over time. This is what an *Energize* Growth® plan can do for you.

The plan provides many benefits, and it builds confidence and credibility. Buyers will believe your growth projections when your written plan is strong, positive, and pervasive enough that it has historically delivered annual increases in profitability. They want to feel confident your company's marketing program will bring in a steady stream of profitable new business in a predictable and controllable manner. They also want to be assured that your plan is *grounded in reality.* (Remember the earlier example of companies who sell solutions looking for a problem?) Sipe advises that "to dramatically increase the value of your company, *you must* implement a systematic marketing program and prove by demonstrated results that it can attract new customers for you and for a new owner" (Sipe 2008, 23).

Assess Your Company's Wealth Quotient

1. How do you regularly ensure that you consistently express and demonstrate your value to the market?

2. To what degree are you handsomely paid for that value (as reflected in your profits, liquidity, cash flow, number of qualified referrals generated, average sales cycles, close rates, and sales predictability)?

3. To what degree do you continuously innovate and reward innovation?

(continued)

(*Continued*)

4. What methods do you employ to focus on business endeavors that do inspire and educate other people? How frequently are these endeavors tracked, measured, and improved?

5. How effective are you at attracting enough of the right clients? In other words, you know who they are, and you market to them in an authentic, consistent, systematic way.

6. How committed are you to endeavors which respect and honor the natural environment?

7. How consistently do you provide your stakeholders, investors, and employees enough time for family, friends, and personal growth?

WHEN IS IT TIME TO EXIT?

Now that you have clarified your WQ, it's time to explore when it makes sense to sell your business. One of the few good lessons that my ex-boyfriend Michael taught me was "Leave the party while it's still fun." This same advice holds true for your business. You can pursue one of three scenarios to leave in a celebratory mood:

1. You can attain a large capital infusion (through private investors, loans, or a buyout).

2. You can sell your company.

3. You can divest shares through an Employee Stock Ownership Plan (ESOP).

Knowing which option is right for you will require time and deep reflection. Consider these questions while evaluating your options.

1. What Is the Opportunity Cost?

Not to challenge Lynne Twist's paradigm here, but we do face *some* limited resources, such as time and energy. I always laugh when I think of my friend Henry DeVries, who jokes "I'm working half days now—only 12 hours!" The true cost of committing a set of resources to one activity is the outcome you could have achieved from committing those same resources to another activity. In other words, there is only so much time, energy, and money available to us at any given point. The opportunity cost of being engaged in your current business might include giving up other resources and experiences, such as:

- Another business venture;

- A more attractive market segment;

- Time for reflection, retreat, and recreation;

- Time spent with family, and friends;

- Diversification of investments;

- Education, intellectual stimulation, or new challenges; or

- Healthy rituals such as travel, exercise, or community activities.

If the opportunity cost of owning a particular business is higher than the overall value received from owning the business, then it's time to seriously consider selling. On the other hand, if you feel that the business is really uplifting and energizing—and it's a profitable way to invest time, talents, and treasury—it does not make sense to sell the business now.

Many people have been so involved in their businesses for so many years that they have a hard time envisioning what life will be like after they exit. However, after a successful sale, the space previously occupied in their life by the business opens up. Many CEOs who said they really wanted to sell their business often reject great offers for a multitude of "reasons." These are just excuses hiding the real reason: they are fearful of losing control of the one thing they know well—and entering uncharted waters.

I sum up opportunity cost this way: is there anything you are currently doing that denies you the gift of free time to explore new possibilities? That alone may be the highest opportunity cost associated with business ownership. You are experiencing high opportunity cost in your business if you hear yourself saying things such as:

- "My business has been good to me. It used to be fun. Now, I'm bored."

- "I could really put more time into this business and turn it around, but I don't want to put any more energy into it."

- "What the heck will I do with the rest of my life?"

- "I put a lot of time into this business. Unfortunately, it distracts me from another venture, with which I think I can have even greater success. This is a great source of income for me, yet I really want to let go of this venture in order to capitalize on the next."

- "We have gone as far as we can with this business based on my talents. The company is well positioned, but we need a new type of leader with a different set of skills and ambitions. That person isn't me. It's time for me to move on. Everyone will be better off if I sold it to a group that could take the company to the next level."

2. How Much Is Enough?

We are fortunate to live in one of the richest countries of the world. As I mentioned earlier, it is seductive to get hooked into the hype that surrounds making money, having more of it than others, and looking good. As a result, we begin to feel that no matter how much money we have, it is never enough. Guess what? Unless you are Warren Buffett or Bill Gates, someone else will *always* have more money than you. Yet, this insidious trap catches many business owners. They just don't realize their current life and economic situation are the envy of 99 percent of the world. On the other hand, when they read about someone else's success, they respond with, "We should be making more money, too."

I see this situation frequently. I meet bright people who own relatively healthy businesses, but they feel discouraged and stuck. Their stories about their current situation and their future are sprinkled with "shoulds" and "oughts." "I *should* do more speaking engagements." "We *ought to* replace my sister-in-law with a more experienced person for that position." They see no end in sight to the achievements they can attain. These mindsets certainly are not the original passion that fueled the business.

These concerns often trigger the ego part of my mind. My ego thinks that it knows a lot more than they do about human behavior. It wants me to dole out advice, which causes me to lose my patience. I just want to say, "Get a dose of reality!" Then my "wise advisor" rescues me. It is incumbent on me to tell the founder, "It is okay to move on. You have invested a lot of your energy in this venture, and you have made *enough money.* Now it is time to let go."

If you find yourself facing a dilemma around this issue, find a quiet place. Turn off your computer and cell phone, and then answer these questions truthfully:

1. Why are we making money?

2. Are we making money in a way that is (still) personally and professionally satisfying?

3. Is this way of making money the highest and best use of our resources and abilities?

4. How would we calculate our opportunity cost, if we have one?

5. How much is enough?

Discuss your responses with your family and trusted advisors. They will lead to a balanced decision about when to sell. Knowing how much is enough is essential to developing a sound exit plan.

The more connected we are to our personal definition of wealth, the less likely we are to succumb to the temptations of our materialistic society. Without a clear sense of your WQ, advertisers, customers, media outlets, credit card companies, and other financial institutions will drive your daily activities and growth decisions. If you're not running your business according to your own wealth formula, you are living someone else's dream.

When I used to visit my parents in Florida, I enjoyed walking along Naples Pier on sunny afternoons. In one particular instance, I remember a fisherman who was really scoring several fish along the pier. Every time he would catch a fish, he measured it against a ruler. If it was bigger than the ruler, he threw it back. Catch, measure, and throw it back. This went on for quite some time. By the end of the day, he threw back quite a few, and a fellow fisherman asked him why. He explained, "The pan I use to cook the fish is only 12 inches wide. I have no use for the bigger fish."

Are you letting opportunities pass you by because you are satisfied with the size of your pot? Or, are your blind spots preventing you from seeing them? Life wants to give us everything; but when we are stuck with our small desires and fears, we are throwing away a prized fish.

Use these new guidelines to reconsider what you want out of your business. Now is the time to re-visit the plan you are using to grow (and potentially sell) your business.

Energy Booster 4

How do we rate our company's current Wealth Quotient, and which of the seven areas needs the most improvement?

CHAPTER 5

The Path to Planning

We must walk consciously only part way toward our goal
and then leap in the dark to our success.

—HENRY DAVID THOREAU

Since I was six years old, getting my pilot's license held a top
spot on my "life goals list." After I had established myself in my
consulting career in 1988, it was time for me to act upon it.

I found the process challenging and exhilarating at the same
time. Acing my landings (and looking forward to "touch and go's")
marked a major milestone. My flight instructor held me to very
high standards, and they paid off. I was a master of checklists
and procedures, and never put myself in dangerous flying conditions. (He later became my husband—but that's a story for another
time.)

The day of my first cross-country solo trip arrived. March 1989
brought cold yet clear days for flying. I mapped my route from
Stratford, Connecticut, to Concord, New Hampshire. The weather
forecast could not have been better. I remember taking off early that
Friday morning. The visibility was perfect. I filed my flight plan
with the control tower at Sikorsky Memorial Airport. My instructor
parked himself beside the radios. All systems were go.

As I passed through Connecticut, then Massachusetts, I could
see New Hampshire on the horizon. My flight charts and vectors
signaled that I was on the right path.

Then something strange happened. The charts told me that Concord had a single runway—yet the airport straight ahead actually had two. I was quite confused.

How could this confusion have happened? I did all the preparation work. My sectional charts were clearly highlighted. My flight plan was impeccable. Things just didn't turn out as expected.

Thankfully, I was flying in a rather rural area and could stop scanning the outside momentarily to reassess my sectional chart. Instead of Concord, I was vectoring to Manchester airport—a bustling controlled airspace! I didn't have their radio frequency, so I was not prepared to call and let them know I was on the edge of their airspace. (This is one of those FAA regulations you don't want to violate.) I took a steep left bank and got out of their airspace as quickly as I could.

I updated my vectors toward Concord and landed safely there. Fortunately, I was only a few minutes late for my estimated touchdown. All was right again in the world.

What does cross-country flying have to do with strategic marketing planning? Just about everything.

If I had skipped over the written plan and developed a loose outline of where I wanted to go, I would have had neither the confidence nor the tools to rechart my course.

Visionary entrepreneurs often tell me that they resist written plans because they don't want to miss out on new opportunities that suddenly appear. Or, they feel stymied by the idea of committing to a vision and set of actions in writing. "Someone might hold me accountable. What if I change my mind later? I lose the freedom to stay flexible." Others tell me that they left a well-paying, yet stifling corporate job because of bureaucracy, inflexible hours, and stringent planning requirements. Developing a written plan evokes those painful memories.

WHY AVOID PLANNING?

Since I began dedicating my career to helping clients successfully implement their growth strategies and create wealthier companies, I have collected a list of the most common stories and excuses for avoiding planning. Here are the top five reasons that company leaders avoid the planning process:

1. *Planning is complex and reserved for large companies.* Over the past year and a half, I have conducted over 50 initial consultations. These prospects generally lead or own companies with annual revenues between $1 million and $30 million. Typically, I begin the conversation with "tell me your top two goals for the next six to nine months." More than two-thirds of them could not answer the question. One woman struggled to answer, then said, "I just don't know how much growth is possible, so I have avoided the question altogether." I informed her that her business had a very low probability of succeeding in the long term.

2. *No heart, all mind.* Well-written plans straddle two worlds: the "what" (as in, "What do we really want our business to look like in one, three, or five years?") and the "how"(as in "How will we get there?"). We focus all of our energy on action steps, because that is our nature. The vision (or the "what") requires deep thinking and removal from daily management activity.

   Furthermore, envisioning the future evokes passion. Visions are activated by the right side of our brain. In many work environments, we use the right brain less frequently than our analytical, task-oriented left brain. When we focus our plan too heavily on activity and it becomes less aligned with our vision, getting everyone aligned to move toward common goals becomes more difficult over time.

3. *I'm too busy working IN the business, so I don't have time to work ON the business.* Michael Gerber, bestselling author of *The E-Myth Revisited,* reports that most entrepreneurs transfer from one full-time job to another. They think that by starting their own business, they are escaping from the trappings of a regular job. They consider themselves very good at their craft, so they hang out their shingle. They become recognized for their talent, so they fill up their calendar with clients. They also become more adept at working IN the business—delivering good service. The downside of this picture is that they choose to invest time in developing their business model. As a result, the business can never run without them. In this scenario, they cannot position the company for eventual sale on favorable terms. Just like their former employer, they are held hostage and hit a growth ceiling (Gerber 1995).

4. *I wasn't involved in building the plan—so why should I support it?* Several years ago, I signed a licensing agreement that gave me rights to teach a well-known business development program. The founder is a genius in her field. As the number of licensees grew, she kept running the business as if she were still flying solo. She made announcements and program changes without ever consulting the licensees. She even decided to double the royalty payments without ever sending out an amendment to the existing licensing agreements. While this was happening and raising our concerns, our requests to be more involved in her growth planning fell on deaf ears. I quickly lost interest in supporting her expansion plans.

5. *If I commit to this plan, I lose the ability to pursue exciting new opportunities.* Let me illustrate this point of view by sharing a childhood story. As a young girl, I attended a private Catholic school in Connecticut. My Mom worked full time at a women's clothing boutique, which was a 15-minute walk

from school. After classes ended, I would meet Mom at the store. One of my favorite pastimes was to stare at the sidewalk and look for shiny coins. Pennies were the easiest to find. Even though they held little value, I loved the idea of finding money and putting it into my piggybank.

Many business owners treat new opportunities the same way. They may have no clue whether the opportunity is going to generate any return on investment, but they love the excitement of finding that shiny penny!

There was the time that Wanda, my client, enjoyed running two companies and helping her husband with his business "on the side." In her primary business, she expanded her team from 3 to 11 full-time employees. She was highly regarded in her industry and won many awards. The area economy was experiencing a major boom, and she capitalized on it. The business grew for nearly 15 years without any written growth plan.

Wanda thought to herself, "This is going well. I love growing businesses and solving problems. Let me see what other businesses I can run so that I can diversify my income stream." She was masterful at finding shiny pennies!

In theory, this made sense. She was energized by the possibility of turning around another business while her existing business was growing quite steadily. Unfortunately, she knew very little about the second business. It was an exciting idea, but a disastrous experience. Three years later, the second business is still barely breaking even and has few prospects of growing. Her primary business also suffered from the diversion. One of her employees embezzled funds from her. New client acquisition growth stagnated. To tide the company over, Wanda was forced to request a higher line of credit from the bank. She finally decided that it was time to extricate herself from that situation. She is currently working on selling the money draining business and refocusing on her primary business.

Don't get me wrong. Luck, persistence, and positive intentions all play a role in growing a profitable company. Wanda has plenty of those qualities. However, as I learned from my cross-country flight, good intentions and persistence are merely complementary skills, not substitutes, for planning.

The main reason to develop a plan is to avoid disagreements, and misunderstandings with some of the most important people to your business—your team. Wanda would have avoided several costly problems if she had developed a written plan with her team. According to Guy Kawasaki, developing a written plan has many benefits.

The right and realistic reasons to write business plans are:

- In the later, due diligence stage of courting an investor, the investor will ask for one. It's part of the game—a business plan has to be "in the file."
- Writing a plan forces the founding team to work together. With any luck, this will help generate a strong, cohesive team. You might even figure out whom you don't want to work with.
- Writing a plan makes the team consider issues that it had overlooked or glossed over in its euphoria—for example, developing a customer service policy.
- Finally, the writing of a plan uncovers holes in the founding team. If you look around the room and realize that no one can implement key elements of the plan, you know that someone is missing. (Kawasaki 2004, 67–68)

Those are powerful benefits, and not very complicated. Yet, few companies ever take their planning seriously enough to realize them. After leading more than 50 planning sessions and 80 strategy reviews in the past decade, I began to get frustrated. I saw these brilliantly developed plans gather dust—often just moments after the planning session concluded. People just ignored them. I wondered why so many highly educated people couldn't implement their plans—and began to doubt my own effectiveness as a strategic advisor.

Were they lacking in education? Did they face language barriers? Were they unable to garner support from their teams? Was the plan inaccurate? Did they forget to involve their key team members? Not at all. None of this was usually true.

The major roadblock that prevented most of my clients from successfully implementing their strategic plans is that *the plans are too complex for anyone to implement and measure.*

That's when I set off on a mission.

I knew both strategic planning and marketing planning are essential components to every company's longevity. Yet, few small to midsized companies plan effectively nor have the time to invest in both processes.

How could I capture the best elements of strategic planning and marketing planning into one model?

What I'm about to share will rock the world of many strategy experts and business professors.

I developed a proven planning system of 11 steps that actually works—and encapsulates the best elements of strategic planning *and* marketing planning. This model does not require you to develop two separate plans to see results.

11 Steps to *Energize* Your Business Growth

1. Strategic market imperatives

2. Consequences and impact

(continued)

(*Continued*)

3. The ultimate result and unique value factor

4. Your ideal client

5. Your elevator statement

6. Your vivid vision

7. Your company values

8. Top growth objectives

9. The gaps

10. "Stop doing" list

11. Measures of success

This chapter focuses on the "outside job" around planning. The first five steps ground your plan in the realities of your market. It is a model that was designed to help companies who want to generate revenues from a preexisting market. It's not an ideal model if you want to be an innovative research laboratory where profits are less critical than the art of innovation.

The next chapter focuses on the "inside job" around planning—steps 6 through 11.

It is easy to write a great strategic plan that contains detailed financials, clear goals, and well thought out assumptions. A balanced, holistic *Energize*Growth® Plan takes a different approach. *It views your universe of possibilities from the outside in, not from the inside out.*

STEP 1. STRATEGIC MARKET IMPERATIVES

We define strategic market imperatives as the internal and external pressures that are driving a need to change. Sometimes we call them business drivers. Review the results from your client and market interviews. What are the drivers that are affecting the respective industries you serve? A number of examples follow:

Internal Pressures

- Internal compliance with company procedures and reporting systems.

- Pressure to align various departments and reduce miscommunications/error rates.

- Reduce time required to assimilate new offices, locations, employees, vendors, or partners.

- Improve accuracy and reliability of reporting processes.

- Develop scalable systems, such as sales processes, financial reporting, or quality control.

- Implement LEAN processes to improve competitive positioning and profitability.

- Position the company for sale or merger.

- Develop or improve employee education, training, and retention programs.

- Maximize customer service or IT capabilities.

- Establish IT security standards.

- Expansion or reorganization of current business partner, channel partner, or vendor programs.

- Streamline time to market.

- Secure additional financing.

- Develop succession plan.

- Relocation, expansion, or downsizing of facilities.

- Position company for special industry award or recognition.

External Pressures

- Leverage capabilities of offshore operations.

- Minimize impact of potential or existing litigation.

- Implementation of new industry standards.

- Compliance with federal, state, or local government regulations.

- Enhance company repute within the community.

- Expand existing market share.

- Be first to enter new markets.

- Build defensive measures against hostile takeover.

- Media positioning strategy (response to negative press, lawsuit, etc.).

- Avert or minimize impact of a natural disaster.

- Protection from potential "employee raids" by competitor.

These are just examples of the strategic imperatives you must consider in your *Energize* Growth Plan®. Some may be short-term imperatives; others may be longer-term. Select the ones that your experience and research tell you are the most urgent.

STEP 2. THE CONSEQUENCES AND IMPACT

Now that you have identified the short-term and long-term strategic imperatives, calculate the impact of each one. Here are the questions you need to answer as specifically as you can. Quantify them to the best of your ability:

1. What is the impact on our clients' *management* teams?

2. What is the impact on our clients' *customers*?

3. What is the impact on our clients' *employees*?

4. What is the impact on our clients' *competitive positioning* or *market share*?

5. What is the impact on our clients' *ability to innovate*?

6. What is the *financial* impact on our clients? (In other words, how will it affect our ability to borrow, expand, merge, exit, or develop new markets?)

7. What is the *total impact* from each strategic imperative on our client?

STEP 3. THE ULTIMATE RESULT AND UNIQUE VALUE FACTOR

The ultimate result-unique value (UR-UV) factor is not just a clever marketing expression. It is one of the most powerful communication tools that you can use in your planning and marketing. It contains four elements:

1. A clear understanding of the issues, problems, or frustrations your clients or prospects are experiencing. What might be missing in their business that they really want to have? What do they *think* the issues and goals are?

2. A clear understanding of what your clients really *need* (not what they want). What do they really need? Note the distinction here. If you are a trusted advisor to your client, you have the ability to ask powerful questions that elicits the real issue, versus the surface issue.

    Let me give an example. I am often asked if my firm provides training. I respond with a question: "What is happening in your business that tells you that you need training?" You can sell them what they want, but it probably won't get them the results they expect. Your job is to uncover the unspoken, hidden issues and aspirations and help the prospective client recognize what they cannot see by themselves.

3. A way to package your solution so that they get what they really want and are extremely satisfied with what you deliver. Packaging your solution is intentionally not a part of your *Energize* Growth® Plan. Why? Because your market cares first and foremost whether you are caring, capable, and competent. If you can make it through this gate, then the method by which you deliver and package your services will most likely be acceptable to them. This is true under one condition: that you are just as caring, capable, and competent after the sale as you were before the sale.

4. A predictable, fail-proof method to reduce the perceived risk of the client doing business with you. Once you are confident that you are working with an ideal prospect, it's your job to eliminate any barriers to doing business with you. It can be as simple as your web site layout. Is your contact information available on every page? Can they find your e-mail address easily? Can you point to a plethora of success stories to prove that you have generated results consistently in the past?

It's not unusual to struggle with articulating your Ultimate Result. Here is a way to gather this information for future clients. Ask every decision maker (the economic buyer, not the "screener" or staffer) in your prospective account these simple questions: *How will your organization be better off as a result of addressing this strategic imperative/goal/objective?* and *"How will you personally benefit from making this problem disappear?"* Their responses will reveal the ultimate results your clients want.

Identifying the total impact of these imperatives can be very eye-opening. Three potential outcomes can emerge: First, you find out what you don't know, and keep researching your market. Second, you determine that you are serving a market that you really don't care much about—and decide to shift company focus. Third, you realize you are undercharging for your services, and immediately determine a way to increase your profit per client.

Your *unique value* is an explanation of how you do things differently from your competition that increases attention and incremental perceived value for your offerings. Discovering your unique value requires a deep commitment to listening. This may be tough for those of you who think that clients hire you primarily for your experience and smarts! You discover your unique value in many ways. All of them are important: a relentless pursuit of client feedback, market research, and the pursuit of innovation. These methods help you discover what makes clients buy from you versus other companies.

According to Samantha Hartley, principal consultant of Enlightened Marketing, "It is not unusual to offer two or three distinct areas of value that, when combined, make your business unique. It may not be just one attribute." She refers to this branding exercise as the "portfolio of benefits" approach (S. Hartley, personal communication, May 13, 2008). We discuss this in greater detail in Chapter 9.

Your internal processes can also be part of your unique value. You may command a premium price because you, unlike your competition, can offer a guarantee. Some services firms offer conditional guarantees, and will not promise specific business results. That's fine, too. This is a more prudent approach to offering unique value. You have no control over certain events, such as a company losing three of their top executives halfway into a project. This can have a severe impact on your ability to promise specific, measurable results or to earn a success fee in lieu of an engagement fee.

Unique value can also appear in other forms, such as:

- Systems that support your team with shared tools, research, templates, and so on;

- Knowledge-sharing culture;

- Superior support staff and internal systems to facilitate communication and delivery;

- A challenging environment that brings out the best at all levels in the organization; or

- Access to skills of others in other departments or disciplines.

STEP 4. IDEAL CLIENT

Once you know the ultimate result (Step 4) that your firm delivers, and you can clearly identify your ideal client, you can confidently communicate what you offer in an elevator statement, or a short sound bite.

Many companies follow a traditional view of their ideal client. They look at market size, company location, demographics, and the level of the decision maker in the organization. In fact, many firms often pursue the same segment as their competitors. This often leads to "me, too" marketing, price competition, and just sheer boredom around marketing.

I use a different strategy with my clients. According to Philip Lay, managing partner of TCG Advisors (www.tcg-advisors.com):

> It is usually better to adopt a contrarian approach and start from the opposite direction than the one that is likely to be adopted by most of your competitors. Therefore, instead of using Dimensions such as physical size, financial parameter, geography, or vertical segment as your *initial* guideposts, I strongly recommend starting with a look at (a) customer organizational *Deportment* (or *behavior*), (b) then industry and market *Dynamics,* followed by (c) industry and business *Demographics* and only at the end, (d) *Dimensions*. Only after you have seen which criteria lead you most directly to a fertile set of potential customers should you give weight to attributes in one or other of the first three groups.

You stand a much better chance of discovering a fertile target segment opportunity that your company can serve effectively if you begin with Deportment and progress through Dynamics and Demographics before focusing your analysis on the more obvious category, Dimensions (Lay 2006).

Here are four aspects of segmentation to expand your thinking about your ideal client—and to attract clients your competitors may not even be approaching.

 The Four Ds of Segmentation

Deportment (Behavior)

- Leadership or management style of the prospective client

- Decision-making processes in the organization

- Adoption strategy of key decision makers (visionary, pragmatist, or conservative)

- Culture of the organization (bureaucratic, decentralized, family owned, etc.)

- In-house resources—existence, professional level, and quantity thereof

Dynamics

- Growth rate of the peer group (i.e., the same industry sector or vertical)

- Competitive pressures

- Expansion, consolidation, or shrinkage of the sector

(continued)

(Continued)

- Regulation or deregulation forces (industry-specific and general, such as Sarbanes-Oxley regulation, OSHA requirements, compliance with Baldrige quality criteria, etc.)

Demographics

- Type of business or function (e.g., wholesale distributor, value added reseller, boutique consulting firm, or online retail store)

- Volume of transactions (few custom projects versus many simple transactions)

- Complexity of business processes (such as quote to order, or invoice to cash)

- Value chain (e.g., wine distributors) or ecosystem (e.g., Toyota automobile dealers)

Dimensions

- Industry verticals or sectors

- Geographic location

- Financial parameters (revenues, profits, market valuation, etc.)

- Physical size (number of employees, subsidiaries/ locations, countries, etc.)

If you are working on a market segmentation exercise, you should expect to look at all of these criteria—and perhaps some that aren't on the list. The ultimate goal is to aim for settling on between four and eight criteria in total. Then see if you can narrow down this list to two or three key ones. This exercise will lower your marketing and sales expenses dramatically, and increase your profitability. You will spend a lot less time chasing troublesome clients who will suck the life out of your resource pool, pay slowly, and require too much hand-holding.

Identifying your *Less Than Ideal Client* is equally as important as identifying your *Ideal Client*.

According to Jerry Vieira of the QMP Group in Portland, Oregon, there are eight different buyer profiles—five of which you want to avoid, and three you should pursue. These traits can apply to individual executives within an account or can be company-wide profiles. Here they are, summarized briefly from Vieira (2007, 4), with the first few types falling into the "must avoid" category:

1. *Stumps* are people with very limited points of view. They are generally not interested in new ideas or changing the way they're doing things. It's hard to get them to see your new approach. Status quo is their favorite option.

   Our team completed a series of interviews with community bank CEOs in 2007. We learned a lot about Stuck-in-the-Mud banks. They believe that traditional approaches are the only trustworthy methods of banking. They see innovation as an unnecessary change—which they fear—rather than seeing it as new and better ways to meet their needs. Many bankers reported that they are "interested in innovation, but don't want to be first." This mindset is what Umpqua Bank's Ray Davis calls "the rubber band syndrome"—there's a rubber band attached to everyone's backside that's connected to tradition, waiting to whip you back to conventional thinking. Umpqua Bank is truly an innovative marketing company that happens to offer banking services. They stand apart from most banks we interviewed.

2. *Takers* are experts at stealing concepts and ideas. They copy your ideas, pass them off as their own, and never give you the credit—or their business. Your inventions and materials may mysteriously show up on their intranet without attribution or your copyrights intact. They love free education.

3. *BMMDIs* (the boss-made-me-do-its) have absolutely no stake in the business, and are only considering your solutions because they were told to—not because they care. They will go through the motions of arranging meetings. You'll find it nearly impossible to identify their personal stake in the success of the project, and they will be unwilling to agree to mutually desirable success measures.

4. *Opportunists* want the absolute base model of your services, at the lowest price . . . and often still expect first-class service. As a result, Opportunists are high-maintenance clients. They also prefer not to be contacted as references. Banks who hang banners offering free gifts with every new free checking account opened may attract Opportunists.

5. *Dreamers* will talk and meet forever to "blue sky it" but rarely get down to practical action steps. Just when you think you have made progress and gained agreement on next steps, they lose focus. They will have moved on to the next new thing.

You can burn a great deal of time with Don Quixote, but never get the sale.

Here are the types of buyers that Vieira recommends you pursue:

6. *Terribly Troubled* folks have a problem or pain and are motivated to fix it. They are desperately seeking solutions and will often make a quick decision due to their sense of urgency. They will be forthcoming with information to help you mutually design a solution—quickly.

7. *Frustrated Drivers* are very interested in the best possible results and will study their options intensively. They will make a prompt decision and are comfortable spending what it takes, but will expect visible results sooner rather than later. Be sure to have comparable clients available for them to contact. They will need guidance on establishing ROI measures and project approaches.

8. *Sincerely Growth Oriented* prospects are already doing things quite well, but want to improve—they are ahead of the curve and want to address potential weaknesses proactively. They want to partner with solutions providers who are innovative and can demonstrate expertise in other industries beside their own. They will often be motivated to invest in your solutions mostly for personal and intangible reasons, such as greater repute, confidence, first to market, and customer image.

STEP 5. ELEVATOR STATEMENT

Now that you have developed a clearer understanding of your ideal client—how they operate, where they operate, and how they think, and how they act—It's time to develop your elevator statement.

An elevator statement clarifies who you help in a compelling way. Robert Middleton of Action Plan Marketing often refers to this as the "audio logo" (www.actionplan.com). No matter what you call it, this simple introduction is the fastest way to grab people's attention and be respectful of their time. I mention repeatedly that people don't generally care what you do—they care about whether you can help them. An elevator statement helps them determine whether your services are appropriate for them. As you share your statement, you are helping them answer the question, "Is this someone I want to keep talking to?" It also earns you the right to have an ongoing conversation. Using your ideal client definition as a springboard, the elevator statement can be very effective at initiating a marketing conversation.

Here is the typical framework:

> We work with . . . (your target audience) who are frustrated/struggling/tired of/fed up with . . . (their issue).

You will know that your elevator statement is effective if the listener says, "Tell me more." It is then, and only then, that you have earned the right to share a story about a client you have helped.

Follow these guidelines to build strong elevator statements:

- Who is your specific target audience?

- What is the biggest frustration they face – or, what is their main aspiration?

Elevator Statement Examples

- *High-end remodeling firm:* "We work with homeowners who have outgrown their current home, and can't bear the thought of moving."

- *Medical clinic:* "You know how frustrating it is today to find preventative health care services? Well, at ABC Clinic, we help people find the best care available."

- *Retail industry consultant:* "We work with retail business leaders who are frustrated by the revolving door of clients and employees."

- *Real estate title company:* "We simplify the overwhelming loan qualification process for homeowners. We eliminate up to 75 percent of the work most real estate brokers are normally forced to do."

How to Develop the Perfect Elevator Statement

An elevator statement is a concise statement that conveys what someone needs to know about your business—in the time it takes to ride up in an elevator. In others words, tell me why I should care in 30 seconds or less. In the professional arena, having an easy-to-understand elevator statement can accelerate the building of your business by years.

The most effective elevator statement and referral development caters to the wants, needs, and tastes of the clients or customers you hope to attract. That means looking at what you offer from their point of view.

To put it bluntly: potential clients or referrers couldn't care less about you and your business (unless you can help meet their agenda). In fact, most of them don't care about

(continued)

(*Continued*)

your educational background, professional experience, or size of your business. They only care about you and your company in direct proportion to your ability to meet their wants, needs, and tastes.

Your job is to make it easy for the people you want to attract to truly understand and appreciate your offering. The easiest way to do it is to break your perfect elevator statement down into simple-to-understand components defining who, what, how, and why:

- Who is your specific target market?

- What are the most important aspects of your offering (from *their* perspective)?

- How do you do it differently from everyone else?

- What specific reason is there to engage you and your business?

Try this exercise: Pretend that you're explaining what you do for your 11-year-old nephew's school project. No jargon or concepts—just simple talk. Then, increase the age level while keeping the simplicity. (Note: It's much harder than it seems.)

After you develop the best elevator statement possible, you should test, test, and test in the marketplace. Once you have formalized your elevator statement, you can limit the variables and really tighten it up. When people start responding favorably, continue with the same message. You may grow tired of it, but keep in mind that future prospects and referring professionals are hearing it for the first time. Even with some repetition, your position gets reinforced in their minds. Stay consistent and reap the full harvest.

So . . . tell me what you do again?

Source: "How to Develop the Perfect Elevator Pitch," by Marc Stein, Vistage International, http://www.vistage.com/featured/how-to-develop-the-perfect-elevator-speech.html. Reprinted with permission.

Marc Stein is president of Everything Communicates, a marketing and business development firm based in Ventura, California.

These five planning steps—Strategic Market Imperatives, Consequences and Impact, The UR-UV (Ultimate Result and Unique Value) Factor, Your Ideal Client, and Your Elevator Statement—are certainly not complex. They do, however, require time and energy. It is time well spent. By viewing your plan from the outside in, you stand a much better chance of developing solutions to preexisting problems and staying clear of the "shiny penny syndrome." You also chart the course for your strategic growth plan for your business. It's a lot like mastering your outside scanning abilities as a pilot. They are not just nice to have; they are lifesavers. Now, let's get on board with the second half of your strategic growth plan—*The Inside Job*—in the next chapter.

 Energy Booster 5

What industry, competitive, market, and client information are we lacking, and how will we find it?

CHAPTER 6

The Inside Job

Your work is to discover your work and then with all
your heart to give yourself to it.

—BUDDHA

Congratulations! You, unlike most of your competitors, just completed five steps in your planning process. You now have a clearer understanding of what you do, whom you do it with, and why you do it. By now, you should feel more energized.

Now it's time to harness that market wisdom and create a wealthy business.

STEP 6. YOUR VIVID VISION

The company's Vivid Vision or vision statement is an emotionally charged, verbal snapshot of what you want your company to be. A vision statement answers "What do I want this business to look like 5 to 10 years from now?" It makes everyone feel energized about the organization's future.

A vision statement needs to follow some simple guidelines. It must be easy to understand by all stakeholders. If your first version of the vision statement is a page or two long, that is okay. In fact, you can even create a picture of what you want to create . . . some companies create collages. In the final plan, however, see if you can distill the vision statement down to a few sentences. People will remember it more easily.

It also works best to write your vision statement in the present tense. This makes others see, hear, and feel the vision as though it has already occurred. In other words, "we will be the world's leading software company" is too fleeting, remote, and cliché for others to feel the vision come alive. Conversely, Microsoft's vision in the 1980s, "We envision a PC in every home running Microsoft software," was much more alive.

In today's time-starved world, the ideal time frame to realize your vision is 5 to 10 years. I have, however, seen organizations create long-term visions quite effectively. Room2Read, a nonprofit agency in San Francisco, California, wants to eradicate poverty through education. Their vision is ambitious and may take a few decades. That doesn't undermine the power of founder John Wood's vision.

A final thought on vision statements. They are not designed as practical targets against which you measure your success or failure. Your goals and strategies will be used for that purpose. Instead, they are designed to open your eyes to what is possible and to elicit emotional commitment from your constituents.

Here are some examples of excellent vision statements:

> We inspire all those we serve with a mission of responsibility and goodness. (Tom's of Maine n.d.)

> We are the first choice of customers seeking the highest value in real estate and service. (JELD-WEN Communities 2008)

Personal vision statements can sometimes consume a few pages. In the business world, however, lengthy vision statements are difficult to remember. As a leader, your goal is to encourage the team to develop a vision statement that is emotionally charged and memorable.

Many companies combine the terms *vision* and *mission*. This is extremely confusing. Avoid doing this at all costs. A mission statement is not an essential piece of your company's growth plan. Mission statements focus on what your company aspires to become within the next three to five years. You typically have one of two motivations to publish a mission statement: you either describe a *situation that needs to change* or an *aspiration of what the organization can become.*

The book of Proverbs says, "Where there is no vision, the people perish." The same is true of your business. Work as hard as you want. Start as many new innovations or projects as you see fit. Post your company's core values in a beautifully framed poster in your office lobby. It won't matter. If these goals and activities are not grounded in a written vision statement, you will never truly harness the hearts and minds of your stakeholders, employees, and clients. You will just employ a set of very busy looking, intermittently effective people.

STEP 7: YOUR COMPANY VALUES

Our values determine the way we run our lives and how we do things at work.

We defined values in great detail in Chapter 2. They form the foundation for your *Energize* Growth® plan. If the plan were a pyramid, your values would form the base.

Here is one word of caution about values. I have seen growth-oriented companies become obsessed about their values. They use them as guideposts to hire, promote, and retain employees. They recruit partners and allies according to shared values. They use them throughout their marketing and branding endeavors. That's great.

Then they begin to expand on their values because the first ones worked so well. Before you know it, the list has grown to a dozen or more. Just remember—we live in an attention-deficient world. Most people will only remember four or five values. Pick your top ones and become adept at repeating them. Ten or more values are worthless. They will only make people think you're academic, self-absorbed, and pompous.

Values are the most effective ingredient to keeping your plan on track. According to Harvard Business School professor and best-selling author David Maister:

> Principles (or values) are the most effective management tools a firm can use. Successful firms are differentiated not by their different goals, clever strategies, or special managerial tactics—these are all remarkably similar worldwide. Successful firms are clearly differentiated by a strict adherence to values, i.e., to professionalism (1997, 2, 75).

Your firm can be said to have values only to the extent that they are clear, nonnegotiable, minimum standards of behavior that the firm will tolerate . . . whether your values are operational (i.e., actually influencing what goes on in your firm) is crucially determined by whether there are consequences for noncompliance.

STEP 8: TOP GROWTH OBJECTIVES

Your vision and values translate into action through your top growth objectives, or TGOs for short. Think of TGOs as a way to bridge the gap between the "What" (vision and values) and the "How" (taking action). Developing your TGOs is a two-phased process. First, you must identify the most important areas of your business that need addressing. These are called *critical goals*. Second, you must clarify some specific, short-term goals that need to be completed that address those key areas. We will refer to these as *SMART goals*. Let's look at critical goals first.

Critical goals are a manageable set of goal categories that will help you fulfill your vision. These are typically categories where your company is weak or lacking resources.

Categories can include:

- Cash flow

- Quality assurance

- IT support

- Marketing planning

- Sales effectiveness or productivity improvement

- Developing inspired, skilled workers

- Product or service packaging

- Marketing

- Low cost delivery

- Distribution in a specific area

- Expanding capabilities in a specific market segment

- People retention

Here is an example. One of our clients, a systems integration company, recently expanded their operations into South Asia. At the outset, things did not go as well as expected. Communications across continents was weak at best. The telecommunications systems often failed. Projects took twice as long as planned. Although the original intent was to maintain project management resources in North America and leverage programming resources in the Middle East, it became a laborious effort. In summary, they were not harnessing the full potential of a global talent pool. Profits suffered. They realized that they needed to do something differently in order to return more acceptable gross margins to shareholders. They established a new critical goal category at their strategic planning session. It was stated as: *"We will develop a passionate, creative, and agile global workforce."*

Another client of ours stays ahead of their competition by raising their standards and often winning industry awards. One of their critical goal categories stated that *"We will raise our customer delight score by completing the Baldrige application process."*

SMART goals ensure that your critical goal categories are addressed at a team and individual level. They are **S**pecific, **M**easurable, **A**ttainable, **R**ealistic, and **T**ime-bound. Each SMART goal supports at least one critical goal category. The time frame should not exceed three to nine months. This allows you to assess and track the success of your goals, and support each person's quarterly performance goals.

Everyone loves the feeling of completing something important and crucial to your company's success. If you can create SMART goals that are attainable within 30 to 90 days, you will make team members highly motivated heroes.

SMART goals become the foundation for the *working business plan* for the organization.

Here is an example of a SMART goal from one of our clients:

Critical Goal 1A: We will develop a passionate, creative, and agile global workforce.

SMART Goal 1A: We will assure that each new employee is fully aware of our vision, values, culture, differentiators, customers, markets, and company procedures within 30 days of their hire.

When I worked for a $1.2 billion company in the late 1990s, I saw this planning process work brilliantly. Every team member had no more than three SMART goals each quarter. One third of my bonus depended on whether I met my SMART goal. If one of my colleagues asked me to work on an assignment that did not help me fulfill one of my quarterly SMART goals, I had three choices:

1. I could invest very little time in that assignment.

2. I could recommend that someone else do it (especially if that person had a SMART goal tied to that project).

3. I could notify my director of the need, develop a new SMART goal, and wait until the next quarter to focus on it.

You can see how this approach can eliminate a huge percentage of the day-to-day firefighting, team conflict, and distractions that are so prevalent in today's overworked, interdependent business cultures. Companies endure economic swings in part when they realize that success is not based on circumstances such as "the economy," but on where they focus their attention, and the goals they choose to pursue.

You can also prioritize your SMART goals using this approach:

1. Write down the SMART goal.

2. Confirm whether that SMART goal links directly to one of your critical goal categories.

3. Is that goal **S**pecific, **M**easurable, **A**ttainable, **R**ealistic, and **T**ime-bound?

4. Test the benefits of that SMART goal by answering this series of questions:

   • What is the benefit to the business owners for pursuing this SMART goal?

   • What is the benefit to your clients for pursuing this SMART goal?

   • What is the financial benefit to your company?

   • What is the personal benefit to management?

   • What is the total benefit of this SMART goal? Write down that figure.

   • What is the impact of *not* doing this? Explore the impact on the market, customers, finances, and management team. Tally up that value and estimated dollar amount.

- What obstacles may prevent you from achieving that SMART goal? These can be financial, people, geographic, cultural, or beliefs that can sabotage that goal.

- What are the solutions to help you overcome those obstacles?

- What are the action steps you can take to accomplish this objective? Assign an owner to complete those action steps.

- Based on the required action steps, estimate the total cost to implement this SMART goal.

- Divide the total benefit by the total cost to implement. Write down the ROI.

- Identify a milestone or metric you will use to measure the success of this SMART goal.

By establishing your top priorities for the next three to six months, you have just completed a major milestone in your company's history. This is no small feat for a growth-oriented company that is seriously considering an eventual sale or merger.

STEP 9. THE GAPS THAT STOP YOU FROM DELIVERING ON THIS VALUE

Gaps are those deficiencies—both psychological and tangible—that undermine your business success. They can include, but are not limited to:

- Your mindset,

- Competition,

- Company culture,

• Management shortage,

• Skills deficiency,

• Financial shortcomings,

• Geographic location,

• Innovation (or lack thereof),

• Lack of information or research, or

• Legal limitations or liability.

Now that I have had the honor to work with more than 300 clients in 12 countries across diverse technology, financial services, and professional services sectors, I can confidently say that planning truly is an inside job. My clients seldom lack intellect or brainpower.

As we discussed in Chapter 2, your success with the *Energize*Growth® system is predicated on your ability to truthfully share your mindset about growth planning—even when it is limiting your growth potential.

The biggest challenge we face as owners of services and knowledge businesses—which most of you lead—is staying in tune with what we love doing, and manifesting that passion at work. This is incredibly important in small to medium-sized businesses. Running the business effectively is important, that's true. But an even more essential quality is ensuring that we constantly pursue things that leverage our passion and talents and monitor things that get in our way. When we forget this important rule, our companies are in serious danger. The first indicator of stagnation is when ambivalence or apprehension sets in, and is ignored.

Begin with the positive mindsets. Which ones have supported your business growth? How do you reinforce them in your company communications and your marketing communications materials?

Zap Those Gaps!

Return to Chapter 2. Write down your answers to these questions:

1. What are your limiting beliefs and mindsets about growing your business?

2. How are you addressing them?

3. How openly do you share them with your team?

4. When they arise, how do you deal with them? What tools or methods do you use to address negative mindsets?

Find a way to anticipate and manage these mindsets—or they will destroy your company.

Now that you have addressed the limiting beliefs that stop you from succeeding, let's review your resource limitations. Think about this as you read the following example and decide whether it rings true for you. One of our clients owns a well-known regional advertising firm. He wanted to grow his monthly revenues from $55,000 to $75,000 within six months. He realized that he was missing a resource—a key team member—to realize that goal. This was preventing him from expanding his client base beyond a certain point. This was because the current creative team was lacking the management abilities to guide the current artist team and handle a large volume of new business.

Your plan may be affected by external forces that are out of your control. Perhaps you have a major global competitor that owns the lion's share of the market. That poses its own set of challenges.

Another resource gap may be an inability to innovate faster than your competition. Several types of innovation can stop you from realizing your growth targets. For example, *revolutionary innovations* introduce products with dramatically improved new features into the market. This is the innovation that most often replaces the incumbent, such as online search engines replacing encyclopedias, or automobiles replacing horse-drawn carriages. In other instances, innovation can simply be disruptive. A *disruptive technology* or *innovation* describes a technological innovation, product, or service that uses a disruptive strategy to overturn the existing dominant market offerings. According to *Wikipedia,* a disruptive technology can sometimes "dominate an existing market by either filling a role in a new market that the older technology could not fill (as cheaper, lower capacity but smaller-sized flash memory is doing for personal data storage today) or by successively moving up-market through performance improvements until finally displacing the market incumbents." Another example, digital photography, is replacing film photography.

It doesn't really matter whether you work within a technical field that undergoes frequent innovation, or whether you practice in a traditional field such as law, architecture, commercial real estate, or accounting. Innovative competitors can strike at any time.

The term *disruptive innovation* was coined by Clayton Christensen, author of *The Innovator's Dilemma* and *The Innovator's Solution.* Christensen replaced *disruptive technology* with the term *disruptive innovation* because he recognized that few technologies are intrinsically disruptive or sustaining in character. He believes that the strategy or business model that the technology enables creates the disruptive impact, *not* the technology itself. This is an important point, and it gets back to what unique value you deliver. Therefore, as a business owner, it is your job to keep focused on the improved outcomes and client delivery mechanisms your innovation creates, not the innovation itself.

It is also your responsibility to be on the lookout for *sustaining innovation* in your industry. This more subtle type of innovation improves the performance of established products. An example would be Intel's or Advanced Micro Devices' continuous stream of new microchips. Each new product creates incremental performance improvement over the prior version.

STEP 10: YOUR STOP DOING LIST

Whoever thought that a stop doing list would be equally important as your *Energize*Growth® Plan? A stop doing list is simply essential. This 11-step process introduces a whole new level of discipline into your organization. It will force you to eliminate activities that you may find interesting, yet they have unproven ROI. Show this list proudly. It gives your team carte blanche to hold your feet to the fire and focus on your plan.

Ever notice how empowering it feels to politely decline when you are invited to a social event? The stop doing list has the same effect. It puts you in control of your business. It raises the performance bar among your teams. In essence, it gives the rest of your organization permission to be discerning.

STEP 11: MEASURES OF SUCCESS

Markets expand and contract. New opportunities arise. Regulations change. Attrition happens. Clients leave. As a result, you'll need to revisit your plans and make changes from time to time. How will you know *when* to make changes to your *Energize*Growth® Plan, and how will you know when your plan is succeeding?

The old adage, "you can't manage what you can't measure," may sound like a platitude—and it is. Unfortunately, I cannot find any company that has grown successfully without formally tracking their progress.

We dedicate Chapter 7 to exploring these dynamics, and helping you identify which metrics will best support your company growth.

Energy Booster 6

What percentage of our teams can clearly explain our vision, values, and elevator statement on the fly?

CHAPTER 7

What's on Your Dashboard?

The brick walls are not there to keep us out; the brick walls are there to give us a chance to show how badly we want something. . . . The brick walls are there to stop the people who don't want it badly enough.

—PROFESSOR RANDY PAUSCH (2008)

If you have been turned off or overwhelmed by the thought of tracking your success, this chapter will calm your fears.

Most of us in the professional world have been seduced by the latest and greatest "success tracking" business paradigms. Every year or two, a sexy new model invades the leading business journals. Some have alluring names, like the "Great Game of Business," the "Net Promoter Score," the "American Customer Satisfaction Index," and the "Balanced Scorecard." I'm certain I've named only a few.

Before you dive into the land of overwhelm, be assured that none of these systems have any meaning—yet. By automatically glomming onto the latest and greatest metrics models, we lose our focus on what really matters. In fact, we often don't know where our company really is; yet we want to measure how the company is doing. In the Western world, we crave information and prefer the most current iteration of it. I call this "Frequent Flyer Syndrome."

It's a malady that you can spot from afar. Have you ever met an executive who leaves on a business trip, reads the frequent flyer magazine on the plane, and stumbles on some cool new idea? She returns to the office and enthusiastically (if not frantically) initiates a new project based on that article. That is one of the ways that salesforce automation took off (couldn't resist the pun!) in the late 1990s and early 2000s. I met many financial executives and vice presidents of sales who read about the technology, and just had to buy some—regardless of whether their company's endeavors warranted it.

As eager as we are to track the right measures and make mid-course corrections, we often set ourselves up for failure. The following demonstrates how that can happen.

Several years ago, I worked with a client in the semiconductor business. My employer had set very aggressive revenue targets for the upcoming year. Since I was a senior partner in the firm, this opportunity represented a significant percentage of my annual target. This client had enjoyed great market success in the late 1990s. Their stock price was skyrocketing. They were hiring across their global locations at a rapid pace. They quickly exceeded $1 billion in revenues, which made the Senior Vice President of Worldwide Sales excited and nervous at the same time. To me, this account represented the article in the frequent flyer magazine—full of promise and opportunity.

The company was losing major opportunities to competitors such as Advanced Micro Devices and Broadcom. They had to do something differently to protect their margins and expand their market share. They realized that developing longer-term relationships and more strategic partnerships with their top 100 customers was a sensible first step. That's when they established a top priority goal: "To increase the effectiveness of our sales organization within one year."

Our firm was selected to help them, and we had a very important mission: to facilitate a shift from being entrepreneurial, transactional "gunslingers," and individual performers to strategic, mature account teams. Their SMART goal fell squarely on the executive team's priority list for the year.

Their Senior VP told us that we had been awarded the business for two reasons: first, because we offered a strong group of experienced professionals who were qualified to help them implement the change across their global operations. Second, we were committed to helping them establish and achieve measureable results. We were not selling them an "off-the-shelf " training program. We were confident that we could make a difference.

When we developed the engagement letter and implementation plan, we mutually established some success measures. The client told us that they wanted to see two key results:

1. A decrease in the amount of time that it took new sales executives to make unassisted sales calls.

2. An increase in the average size sale per customer. In their mind, this would be a direct result of the sales teams' improved ability to qualify, pursue, and win larger business opportunities.

The initiative was scheduled to launch at the firm's worldwide sales conference in Cancun, Mexico. People were excited because this was the first real sales recognition event in the company's history. We wanted to be sure that kickoff session went flawlessly, so we coached the Senior VP on how to effectively announce the new program. After all, their director of sales operations' career was tied to the success of this engagement.

We prepared extensively for the conference and became confident in the sales development plan. Then things abruptly went south. The Senior VP stopped showing up for our scheduled meetings. The director of sales operations was hastily reassigned to other projects, and then laid off within just a few months. The entire Cancun conference was cancelled, leaving sales teams confused and demoralized.

What *really* happened here? If we had looked more closely, we would have known that the client's measures of success were arbitrarily selected and ran contrary to their company culture and their stage of growth at that time. The evidence was there—we just chose to ignore it. This organization hired and promoted engineers and inventors. Even the board of directors was mostly comprised of retired engineers. They prided themselves on innovation and being first to market. At that stage in their history, they were clearly enjoying life in the "technology tornado"—high growth, spotty hiring practices, cash flow challenges, and broken business processes. The idea of shifting the culture from a product innovation focus to a customer intimacy focus was a tall, if not impossible, order.

I can also remember the emotions that the teams experienced. The salespeople were busy, but relaxed. They were proud of the first few major accounts that they closed. The human resources and operations groups were overtaxed and trying to keep up with the hiring pace. The company outgrew its customer relationship management and production tracking software systems.

Our sales initiative clearly required major changes in how the teams behaved and operated. Since the Senior VP was never truly committed to make the necessary changes to move the teams in that direction, we had set ourselves up for failure. We didn't see the warning signs, and the project evaporated. Within just a few years, the company stock price plummeted from over $200 to less than $10 per share.

In hindsight, we realized that our mistake had been saying yes to a client without truly understanding what phase of growth they were tackling. The success measures we had mutually established were meaningless.

Several years subsequent to this discouraging turn of events, I met Marc Johnstone, CEO of Shirlaws Coaching in San Francisco, California. I wanted to better understand why so many companies ignore the phase of growth they are in, and why they often jump to setting arbitrary success measures. Since Marc's firm works with over 400 clients, and employs 200 business coaches worldwide, I knew that he could provide some insight into this situation.

The way in which Shirlaws describes the five stages of business growth with their clients is essential for several reasons. First, they help create a context for knowing what phase of business growth a given company is experiencing. Second, the company will see an immediate connection between the emotions of their employees and the plateaus (or metaphorical brick walls) that they're hitting. Finally, this growth chart will help the group identify which actions are necessary, based on what phase of the business cycle they're experiencing. Shirlaws refers to these as "platform issues" like capacity planning, sales processes, and client services; and "growth issues" such as succession planning, market positioning, distribution, vendor relations, or strategic alliances (Shirlaws 2005, 3). This model helps anchor your entire team in a common understanding of where you are—and what needs to be done to move forward in a positive way.

As you review the stages (Figure 7.1), listen for the emotions, behaviors, and key indicators that you typically experience during each stage:

1. Startup

2. Growth

3. Advanced growth

4. Plateau

5. Decline

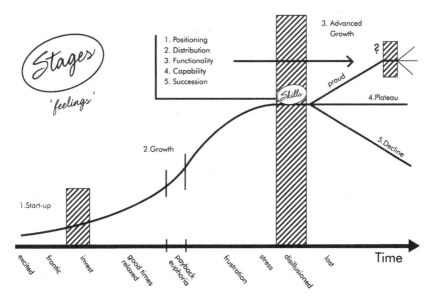

FIGURE 7.1   Shirlaws' Stages of Growth

Source: Marc Johnstone, Navitas Ltd. Reprinted with permission.

In the *startup stage,* business owners experience euphoria, excitement, and frantic emotions. New clients sign up for your services. You establish a web site for the first time. Marketing may be a foreign notion to you. You attribute many of your opportunities to luck or favors from old colleagues.

If you can make it through startup, prepare to hit your first brick wall. You find that your business is revolving completely around *you.* Although you have proven that your business model is viable, your business functions are fuzzy. In other words, people run around performing "cover-your-behind" activities because a high percentage of them have poorly defined jobs. In fact, they usually cannot explain how their jobs tie directly to your company's goals. Some job functions may overlap. When it's time to buy new computers, you involve everyone in the process. The evaluation takes much longer than expected, and may even sit in your inbox for several months without moving forward. Inefficiencies abound—from the mailroom to the marketing department.

You now face a difficult choice. You can either invest further in the business—and spend your time, effort, and money in developing your infrastructure—or you can continue to immerse yourself and your company in daily business operations and enjoy the adrenalin rush of frantic excitement. By choosing the first option, you can successfully scale the first brick wall.

After conquering this obstacle, you are entering the *growth stage.* You know it because you start to feel more relaxed. You are hitting your stride. You have enough cash to purchase that vacation property or fancy watch. Your company is generating healthy financial returns. You feel like your efforts are finally paying off. Your small team actually understands how their jobs tie directly to the success of the organization. You see few to no political battles and turf wars. Work is fun again!

During the growth stage—perhaps for the first time in your company history—you experience joy in your business. You celebrate industry awards, a steady stream of referrals, and community recognition. Your teams enjoy spending time together at social and sporting events. You're hoping that the ride continues.

Unfortunately, it seldom does. You just landed some big clients, and your business feels as if it doubled overnight. Your emotions shift from joy to frustration and stress because your company is not positioned to handle the increased workload. Instead of pausing to reflect on the ideal strategic moves and investments, you immediately go for broke. You hire quickly and ramp up your operations. You expand offices and buy more equipment. Cash flow is strained.

Even though you are establishing a solid foundation for your new hires, you're growing impatient because they can't seem to keep up with the workload. That new software migration just doesn't meet your expectations, and you learn about cost overruns from your IT department. Your infrastructure is holding on by a thread.

Congratulations—you have hit the second brick wall. You now feel disillusioned, apprehensive, stressed (again), and lost. Your emotions are beginning to rub off on your teams. Your best people—those whom you recruited away from some of the finest companies—are disillusioned. They start leaving for more "stable" positions, or venture out on their own. They feel that they have no stake in the company's future, and the cost of replacing them is skyrocketing. This growth spurt needs to be managed—and quickly.

As you are leaning precariously against the second brick wall, you might be tempted to stop *delegating* and start *abdicating*. This is a common coping mechanism, and it's important to understand the distinction between the two. Instead of empowering other team members to complete the tasks for which they are accountable, you completely surrender all supervisory responsibility and assume that they will do a great job. You are tired and stressed, and you simply don't have much energy left to properly delegate and manage your teams through the rapid growth.

I once worked with a CEO of a global training company who proved to be a master abdicator. On the surface, Joanna had a well-run business, and appeared to run a company that was operating squarely in the growth stage. They were expanding at 15 to 20 percent per year. They were slightly profitable and professional-looking to the outside world. Joanna commanded five-figure fees at major industry conferences and sold thousands of books. Yet something didn't seem right to me, so I kept asking questions.

For example, I inquired of Joanna: "Tell me how you track your team's performance on a regular basis." "Show me the process you use to hire and retain people." "You said you only want to work three days a week within the next five years so that you can train for triathlons. Walk me through your succession plan." No matter what the question, Joanna provided the same answer: "Ann handles that for me. . . . Barry manages that; I don't know. . . . You will have to ask my finance manager for that information."

Joanna was not running a growth business. She was abdicating her responsibilities to various other members of her organization. She was leaning against the second brick wall, and she didn't know it.

I offered Joanna three options to break free from her abandonment style of leading:

1. *Accept the growth plateau you have reached, collect your large paycheck, and be grateful.*

2. *Be prepared to watch the company decline or die.* By relinquishing this much control, you are losing the ability to proactively and skillfully anticipate problems.

3. *Hire a professional CEO to help you design a new growth strategy. Long term, this will enable you to experience both cultural and commercial success.* Find an approach that will restore your joy for the business. For example, you can extend your training programs to new markets. You can offer new services to your existing clients. You can establish new joint ventures. Re-defining your role in the business can breathe new life into it.

Scaling the second brick wall takes focus and patience. In fact, Shirlaws finds that the process typically takes five to seven years. The founders must agree to invest in five key areas to ensure business continuity and advanced growth:

1. *Reposition the company.* Positioning relates to how a company differentiates itself in the eyes of their customers, and provides focus for the business model and all related activities.

2. *Develop solid distribution and referral systems.* Distribution is about creating and maintaining referral relationship channels in the market so that the company frees itself from the traditional direct sales approach.

3. *Define and strengthen the company's functionality.* This looks at how your company allocates its resources across the three key areas—strategy, operations, and infrastructure—and then getting the right people doing the right jobs. Operations relates to revenue-generating activities such as sales, manufacturing, product delivery, client service, and marketing. Infrastructure relates to overhead costs such as accounting, information technology, facilities, human resources, legal, compliance, and administration.

4. *Expand your capabilities.* Possibly for the first time in the company's history, you must focus on hiring people for their skills and track record, not on personality, tenure, family ties, or friendships. Capability refers to the quality and breadth of skills in the organization.

5. *Build a succession strategy that centers on hiring top performers—not on the founder's eventual exit.* The focus is on building a strong "A team" so that the founder's exit is successful, if not uneventful.

If a company succeeds at putting these items into place, they will enter the *advanced growth* stage. Here, you and your teams will experience one of two emotions. You will either feel energized and proud of the company's vision, or lost and confused about how your position contributes to the company's future direction. Expect both reactions. According to Johnstone, "After spending a few months or years in advanced growth, you can expect to hit another brick wall and begin the growth planning process all over again" (M. Johnstone, personal communication, September 16, 2008).

If your organization is unable or unwilling to implement these five key systems, you will experience the *plateau stage,* where you will feel a sense of contentment that may last temporarily. Another *brick wall* will appear, and you will face the same dilemma once again. You will be faced with many options—in fact, too many to consider. Once again, anxiety sets in. If you do not succeed at establishing the five systems, you will eventually experience the final (and least favored) stage: *decline.*

During decline, you will notice that people are not innovating as well as they used to. You start to wonder if this hard work and effort was really worth it. You operate in survival mode. New client acquisition slows to a trickle. You feel defeated and tired.

Your awareness of these stages—and your ability to educate your teams on how to use it—can make a difference between growth and extinction. Here are some basic guidelines to remember as you apply this stages chart to your business:

1. *It is difficult to estimate how long each stage will last.* I have met CEOs who were stuck leaning against the first brick wall for several years and who had become paralyzed. Their business was primarily their personal ATM machine. On the other hand, some companies move swiftly through the second brick wall within just two or three years. They do so by investing in several areas—such as repositioning themselves in the market, improving and streamlining distribution, developing their bench strength for succession, hiring on credentials versus personality, and so forth.

2. *The model forces you to view growth through the lens of emotion, not scientific data and metrics.* Some of you will not be comfortable with this approach; however, it's important that you attempt to embrace this viewpoint. Your only other option is to return to Industrial Age thinking by believing that strategic growth is fundamentally an analytical, left-brained exercise that doesn't involve the human component.

3. *If your company is owned by several partners or family members, you have to let each person work through the process.* Every partner may experience different feelings; hence, they may view the company at a different stage than another person.

This book focuses on helping companies minimize the pain and effort required to move through three stages of company growth: the first brick wall after startup is achieved, growth, and the second brick wall after growth. The manner in which you measure success will be different as you move from one stage to the next. It's up to you to decide which measures are worth considering and to see how each applies to your business. The next chapter will help you do exactly that.

Energy Booster 7

What stage of growth are we experiencing, and what can we do to scale the next wall?

CHAPTER 8

Design Your Dashboard

Those who stand for nothing fall for anything.
—ALEXANDER HAMILTON

Before you try to pick the perfect success measures, temporarily shift your focus away from our traditional "trailing" indicators. These may include sales, gross margin, and revenue per employee. Focusing heavily on these indicators is like flying an airplane by constantly looking over your shoulder instead of determining what's in your flight path.

Your job as CEO is different from the CFO or controller. Your job is to create top line growth, ensure profitability, and develop a happy, engaged team. Retired CEO and consultant Kraig Kramers recommends that you focus on metrics and behaviors that tell you how you are progressing in these areas—which you can refer to as key performance indicators (KPIs), or just key indicators. Just be sure that everyone on your team uses the same terminology. These are the causes, drivers, and contributors to your end results.

Over one thousand companies have used Kramers' tools. He suggests that focusing on the following priorities—listed in order from most to least important—will substantially increase your chances of creating a predictable growth machine:

1. *Clients:* Knowing what causes sales to consistently happen—*not* tallying profits—is your company's number one priority. As you navigate through each growth stage, you need to dedicate a solid percentage of your time to clients.

2. *Growth:* Although CEOs talk a good game about growth, they don't view it in a systematic way. Even fewer link growth measures to their success dashboard. Kramers claims, "Companies often react to growth in one of two ways: they either let it happen randomly, or passively let it happen with no strategy in place. Then they hire and fire people sporadically, depending on the unanticipated growth rate" (K. Kramers, personal communication, August 8, 2008). The cost of replacing an employee costs companies at least 150 percent of the person's annual salary (Allegiance n.d.). This seat-of-the-pants planning and hiring approach has a significant impact on the company's morale and long-term growth potential. Growth can reliably be measured in three ways:

   • *Units:* Also known as sales volume, number of new clients month over month, and so on.

   • *Dollars:* The total amount invoiced and collected.

   • *People:* Kramers ensures that every dashboard includes tangible and intangible methods to gauge employee happiness. Although employee satisfaction surveys can be a helpful barometer, you can also conduct informal interviews and conversations and learn a great deal. Your client satisfaction surveys should also measure the consistency of the selling, purchasing, and support experiences. These can tell you a lot about how employee enthusiasm and happiness affects what causes sales.

3. *Cash:* Every CEO is responsible for managing cash. Kramers recommends that you develop a system to view your cash position on a daily basis. This will help you make friends with your banker during recessionary times. It will also prompt you to anticipate potential cash flow issues well before they become a crisis.

4. *Profits:* Compared to the other four factors, profits are the only metrics that are *results,* not *drivers,* of financial discipline. One of the best ways to assess your profitability is by finding research that shows comparable profit ranges of your peers and competitors. As mentioned in a previous chapter, tools such as ProfitCents from SageWorks can help. But keep in mind that when leaders obsess about profits at the expense of clients and growth, they will drive the wrong behaviors among their direct reports. For example, what will you do if a salesperson chooses to cut corners while serving one of your key clients in order to reach current profit goals? The answer is obvious: it is a disaster waiting to happen—unless your company is in decline and doesn't care about retaining clients. Reducing the cost of sales at the expense of upsetting your top clients and damaging your brand is not the ideal option.

Key indicators—much like the *Energize*Growth® Plan—help you focus on the right activities: generating revenues with ideal clients. Notice that profits don't grow the business—marketing and sales do. These are the primary activities that will contribute to what I refer to in Chapter 4 as your company's Wealth Quotient—the customers, growth, and people that contribute the most to your company's longevity, vitality, brand equity, and future market cap.

Identifying your key indicators may evolve by asking for feedback. Kramers recommends that the CEO spend twenty minutes per day walking around the office, and asking very specific questions of employees on how the team thinks things can improve, so that your most important metrics are attained. This builds confidence and trust in the KPIs.

Kramers also believes that CFOs and CEOs should be viewing different dashboards: the CEOs should reflect key indicators (internal and external behaviors) that fuel the trailing indicators (internal and external measures/results). CFOs should consider using a dashboard that tracks more traditional metrics, such as cash flow, employee attrition rates, and gross margin. This is an approach you may consider.

Kramers offers a great example of how companies have successfully implemented performance measurement tools. He had a homebuilder client who hired him to refine their success measures. Kramers ended up designing two dashboards: one for the CEO (Figure 8.1), and one for the CFO. The CEO dashboard contained eight charts which contained key (or leading) indicators, and asked questions like: How many people visited their model homes? What was their reaction after they toured the model home? For the CFO, he tracked the traditional measures.

The benefits from developing your dashboard appear quickly. People feel happier because they can see how their jobs and actions tie to your key indicators. Second, they witness an improvement in profits and revenues.

Most people are unaware of the key indicators that they should track. This depends on what growth stage your company is experiencing. As your business matures over time, so will your success measures. Consider several general key categories as a starting point as you develop your own indicators. You'll be able to see which ones map directly to your maturity level as you dig more deeply to create meaningful measures. Table 8.1 shows some examples for you to consider.

WHY DASHBOARDS BREAK

If you begin to feel excessively confident or over-reliant on your newfound key indicators, beware! Dashboards can give you a false sense of security. If you think they are the ultimate source of predicting customer loyalty growth, you will be disappointed—and your dashboard will break.

Just ask Paul Spiegelman, CEO of the Beryl Companies in Dallas, Texas. This 24-year-old private company provides award-winning outsourced call center services to over 500 hospitals across the United

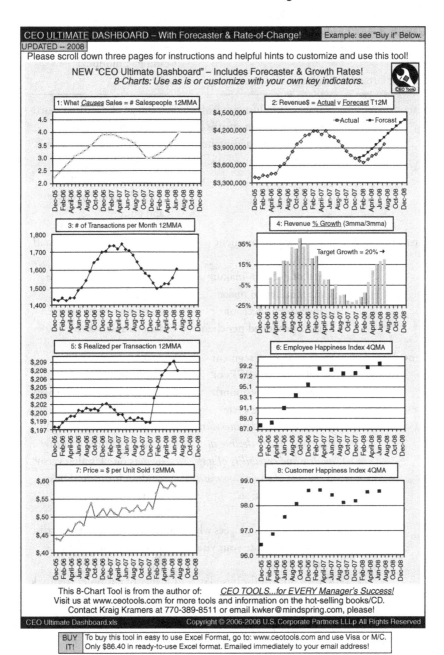

FIGURE 8.1   CEO Tools Ultimate Dashboard

Source: Kraig Kramers, www.ceotools.com. Reprinted with permission.

TABLE 8.1   Leading and Trailing Indicators by Growth Stage

Stage of Growth	Trailing Indicators	Leading/ Emotional Indicators
Start-up	Number of industry awards Number of design awards Speed of market acceptance Rate of new client acquisition	Percentage of decisions based on emotion (high) Acceptance rate of company message or brand Energy level of founders Clarity of company values and culture
First Brick Wall	Cash flow improvement percentage Speed of decision making Time required to make investment decisions Dollars generated per client	Level of commitment of staff (nonowners) Confidence levels to move forward Level of alignment between actions and words
Growth	Share of market segment Number of new RFPs or leads per week/month Length of selling cycle Available cash (*declines during this phase due to decline in quality and capability of staff as the rate of growth increases*) Market penetration per segment Percentage of employees who can clearly state your vision and values Rate of growth for business expansion ideas and strategies Customer Happiness rating Employee Happiness rating	Style of decision making (confident, relaxed) Percentage of decisions based on facts and supported data (*should be growing*) Percentage of time spent by owners on planning versus random hiring and busy work Number of marquis clients Ability of team to instill trust and confidence in the market Quality of customer feedback generated for future growth decisions (*declines when growth accelerates*)
Second Brick Wall	Number of net new employees	Quality of employees retained

TABLE 8.1 (*Continued*)

Stage of Growth	Trailing Indicators	Leading/ Emotional Indicators
	Order fulfillment error rates	Number of times that media or market invites you to speak on your expertise
	Percentage completion of strategic initiatives	Level of alignment between your business values and team actions/decisions
	Percentage investment in infrastructure (should increase)	Percentage of CEO's time spent on developing and expanding "A team" versus personal succession planning
	Number of fun and celebration events per month	Increase in *blame game* behaviors (the economy, family, employees)
	Consistency of delivery	
	Percentage of decisions relying on principals (will increase during this phase)	
	Gross margins	
	Profit margin	
	Growth in leads generated through word of mouth (e.g., blogs, media coverage)	
Advanced Growth	Retention rates of top performing employees	Level of innovation and excitement among leadership team
	Client satisfaction ratings	Level of team alignment
	Number of new market/product launches	Ability to manage confusion among lost employees (who do not see a link to their roles in the new company vision)
	Health of Culture Index	Percentage of succession/exit plan completed
	Rate of new marketing initiatives	Quality and depth of second in command team
	Rate of new innovation/product launches	Level of pride

(*continued*)

TABLE 8.1   (*Continued*)

Stage of Growth	Trailing Indicators	Leading/ Emotional Indicators
Plateau	Retention rate of best clients Gross margin percentage	Level of overwhelm due to influx of new ideas Project completion rate (declining)
Decline	Growth in tactical versus strategic decision-making activity Revenue growth (drops)	Increased desire to sell Level of tiredness Survival mode Focus on downsizing or position to be acquired

States. They have experienced double-digit growth for over seven years, and have expanded to over 350 employees. Five years ago, Paul's company hit the second brick wall stage. He did not recognize this because of a change in the company's financial measures; rather, he noticed it because of changes in employee behavior. Departments began operating like silos. People did not appreciate each other. And as they grew apart, people became more inept at understanding what other departments actually did.

Spiegelman realized that in order to scale the second brick wall, his company needed to establish concrete ways to measure success. They implemented the Balanced Scorecard™ tool, and immediately experienced several benefits. For one thing, they began to focus on three-year goals versus quarterly performance and firefighting during their quarterly executive sessions. Says Spiegelman:

> The one page dashboard helps bring me up to speed very quickly on what's happening in the business. Furthermore, my teams have a much greater understanding of how their activity rolls up into the departmental and company-wide values and vision. This translates into greater employee loyalty. In addition, our profitability has continued to

outpace our revenue growth for the past four years, and our profits are nearly six times higher than the public companies in our industry. But it's just as important to look closely at my company's cultural thermometer. There is an absolute correlation between my people's mood and our financial metrics (P. Spiegelman, personal communication, September 11, 2008).

In Figures 8.2 and 8.3, Spiegelman shows in a simple, yet elegant way, how to align your strategic plan with the appropriate success measures.

Observing and anticipating internal behavior changes is the sign of a great leader. Imagine what you can learn by applying those same skills to your client relationships. Would client loyalty increase? Not necessarily. A recent *Sloan Management Review* article reveals

FIGURE 8.2   One Page Strategic Plan

Source: Paul Spiegelman, The Beryl Companies. Reprinted with permission.

		Develop a technology vision	Implement product ownership and	Improve internal business processes	Improve internal training	Aggressively manage the Beryl Brand
Customer	Create & implement the Beryl brand strategy					😐
	Expand Beryl's strategic role with clients & the market					☺
	Achieve new product sales					☹
	Leverage *The Beryl Institute*					😐
Learning & Growth	Enhance learning & growth for call advisors			☺	☺	☺
	Enhance learning and growth for non-call advisors			☺	☺	☺
	Establish a Beryl onboarding program			😐	😐	😐
	Recruit new positions & talent	😐	☺	☺		
Internal Business Processes	Develop a centralized implementation function		☺	☺		☺
	Develop a centralized QA funciton	☹	☹	☹		☹
	Develop a product management function		☺	☺		☺
	Develop a technology vision & strategy	☹	☹	☹		
Financial	Maintain profitablity	☺	☺	☺	☺	☺
	Increase revenue year over year	☺	☺	☺	☺	☺
	Keep the clients we have (retention)	☺	☺	☺	☺	☺

FIGURE 8.3   Sample Balanced Scorecard

Source: Paul Spiegelman, The Beryl Companies. Reprinted with permission.

why several customer loyalty experts have misled business leaders:

> Most companies do a relatively poor job of managing their relationship with their customers. It isn't that they don't care, but rarely do they have any insightful information they can act upon to make the relationship more valuable. As a result, understanding how customers perceive the relationship and anticipating what they will do is typically no more reliable than reading tea leaves.

They then deliver the sobering news—the news that would make customer loyalty experts cringe:

> In recent years, researchers have advanced a number of customer metrics to illustrate the connections between customer behavior and growth. In the harsh reality of the marketplace, however, these efforts have generated more smoke than heat... none of them have shown themselves to be universally effective across all competitive environments (Keiningham, Aksoy, Cooil and Andreassen 2008, 2).

As a business leader, your need to remain flexible and adaptive is paramount. Do not delegate full responsibility of gathering client feedback to your vice president of marketing or vice president of sales. Not every client loyalty and growth issue is a marketing problem, nor can every metric—including the ubiquitous customer satisfaction metrics—be tracked by launching an impersonal online survey. The client experience, political trends, changing cultural norms, and other variables can skew even the best key indicators.

Here are the first steps to putting your success measures into practice:

1. *Using the growth stages model and descriptions, honestly determine what phase of growth your company is experiencing.* There are no wrong answers—only truthful ones.

2. *Develop a list of success measures that may apply to your business in this growth phase.*

3. *Using the growth versus indicators chart, build a list of 10 to 15 meaningful success measures.* Brainstorm with your strategic partners and employees to develop a comprehensive list. Thank them for their input and time.

4. *Validate your final list of success measures with your executive team, accountant, and sales teams.* Be sure the list contains

eight or fewer measures. You will not have the time—nor the energy—to track more than eight.

5. *Determine a method to track those measures.* You will find options from www.ceotools.com and recommendations from the Balanced Scorecard Institute (www.balancedscorecard.org) to start the process. Over one hundred companies sell software tools that are based on the Balanced Scorecard performance management methodology. Alternatively, ask your accountant to recommend some tools. You can also post a question on Google Answers or LinkedIn to find out what companies similar in size or location are using.

6. *Assign owners who will report progress against those measures on a regular basis.* Owners may include your bookkeeper, vice presidents of development and sales, accountant, CFO, controller, or a combination of these people. Be sure that their performance plan and bonus are tied to this important task.

7. *Set meaningful goals that contribute directly to your success measures.* Make sure your teams have bought into those goals. Every team member should have no more than three goals per quarter. They normally will contribute to one of your key indicators. Once you have achieved this, your team members will see more clearly how their jobs tie directly to the success of the company. They will be more internally motivated to support growth. This sounds like an overstatement of the obvious, yet survey after survey has revealed that most businesses fall woefully short of establishing meaningful goals with their teams.

8. *Communicate your goals at least 10 times in order to build trust.* This has to be done in a credible, authentic way. Walk the four corners of the building for 20 minutes per day, and tell your teams, "I value your opinion. How can we make our client experience better? How can we make our people

work together more closely? What suggestions do you have for celebrating our success this year?" Listen to and heed their results and, most importantly, acknowledge when you've put one of their ideas into practice.

9. *Regularly check your "cultural thermometer."* Maintain programs that keep people happy and energized. Find what makes them tick, and continue to find ways to help their work fulfill those aspirations and motivators.

10. *Track progress publicly and in small increments.* Find a way to announce your progress to your teams and close allies. For example, if you want to grow your revenues from $10 million to $12 million within one year, translate that into a visual representation that breaks down that goal into $2 million over 12 months. Post a poster or dashboard where everyone can see it, and celebrate your progress by updating it monthly. Remember—this will activate the Reticular Activation System (RAS) in people's brains and condition them to see the positive results already happening.

What Growth Measures Matter?

1. Review the questions that follow.

2. Identify what actions you can take to get the missing information.

   What is your *number one* key indicator?

   _____

   _____

   _____

   _____

(*continued*)

(*Continued*)

What are your CFO's key indicators?

_____

_____

_____

_____

What *percentage of your resources* (budget/people) are moving you toward that goal?

_____

_____

_____

_____

What milestones and activities prove that?

_____

_____

_____

_____

What percentage of your team is *rewarded and aligned* to ensure they focus on that result?

_____

_____

_____

_____

Tracking the appropriate leading and trailing indicators will help you make clear choices that your team can understand. They give you a common foundation to communicate, track, and celebrate the achievement of your plan. Remember, too, that the *Energize* Growth® Plan does not replace a lengthy, strategic planning process for mature, diversified, global companies. That is not its intent. The goal is to provide you with four key capabilities as a business leader:

1. A common framework for thinking about your business;

2. A method for staying grounded in market realities and needs;

3. Alignment of your teams around common goals; and

4. A way to pursue high return opportunities with less effort, arm-twisting, and unnecessary conflict.

David Van Seters, CEO of SPUD, understands the value of using a success dashboard. SPUD is the first online organic grocer to actually report a profit, and will reach nearly $25 million in revenues this year. Headquartered in Vancouver, Canada, SPUD is reinventing the way people look at healthy living and grocery delivery services. Van Seters' measure of success is based on a "sustainability scorecard." Says Van Seters, "We make enough of a profit to fulfill our 'triple bottom line' promise. First, we focus on the environmental impact of our business. Second, we constantly look for ways to improve our social performance. Finally, we provide a return to our investors." The results are still playing out—SPUD intends to expand from 7 to 24 cities within the next five years. Their true key indicator is customer feedback. One of their regular customers told Van Seters that ordering groceries from SPUD "is like getting free Karma with every order" (D. Van Seters, personal communication, September 12, 2008).

If this general outline can help you stop pursuing just one time-wasting venture, then it will have served its purpose. Think of your success measures within the *Energize* Growth® Plan as the global positioning system (GPS) for your business. These 11 steps won't fly the plane for you and guarantee growth. They won't make headlines in the next issue of your favorite frequent flyer magazine. Nor does a written plan prevent you from performing periodic maintenance. But it sure will keep you on course.

Energy Booster 8

Which success measures really count, and how will we track them?

CHAPTER 9

Plan Your Brand

> Nothing can add more power to your life than
> concentrating all your energies on a limited set of targets.
> —NIDO QUBEIN, www.nidoqubein.com

This book should come wrapped in a warning label.

By now, you have read enough chapters to know this book is for risk takers. Rule number three in Chapter 1 said that in order to succeed, you have to be willing to take risks and kiss the status quo goodbye. Your own company identity will be challenged, if not changed forever, after you implement the planning steps I have outlined.

Chapter 4 provides seven principles to help you increase your Wealth Quotient (WQ). This most likely redefined your previous perspective on how to build a truly wealthy business. The first WQ principle forms the cornerstone for this chapter: *You consistently and confidently express and demonstrate your value to the market.* This is one of the only ways you will ever attract enough of the "right" clients—in other words, you know who they are; you can explain your ideal client to others very clearly; and you market to them in an authentic, consistent, systematic way.

Are you scared yet?

Without a clear understanding of branding, and a willingness to challenge your current brand, your company's *Energize* Growth® Plan will never tap into the emotions that cause clients to buy from you.

Your brand is the sum total of all "touch points" and experiences that your clients, employees, and community have when they

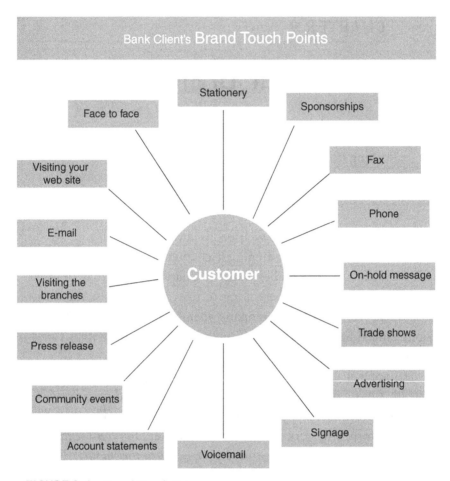

FIGURE 9.1   Brand Touch Points

Source: Shawn Solloway. Reprinted with permission.

interact with you. Shawn Solloway, president of EXIT Marketing sums it up nicely: "We use the *Brand Touch Points* tool to show clients all the areas that they interact with clients and prospects. We encourage them to accurately and consistently reflect their positioning at all these points. Everything matters." They developed the tool in Figure 9.1 for one of their private banking clients (S. Solloway, personal communication, September 12, 2008).

HOW TO WASTE MONEY ON BRANDING

Branding doesn't have to be expensive—but there are times when it just doesn't make sense to do it. Do *not* worry about your brand during two phases of your company life cycle: startup and decline. According to Scott Bedbury, consultant and author of *A New Brand World:*

> [T]he best brands never start out with the intent of build-ing a great brand. They focus on building a great—and profitable—product or service and an organization that can sustain it. Once that has been accomplished, you can slam your foot on the marketing accelerator and let the whole world know about it. But get ready to meet the de-mand created by that marketing or you will destroy your brand before it ever gets off the ground. (Bedbury 2003, 11, used with permission)

In other words, if you embark on a brand development project too early in your company's history, you may be wasting time and money. During the startup phase, spend the time gathering and writing great client case studies. Here you are looking for patterns in their behavior and emotional response—but you are not yet ready to create a pithy positioning document. During decline, you will probably be preparing to sell your business in a hurry (probably in two years or less). Investing five or six figures in a branding exercise may yield you nominal financial upside or client goodwill.

NINE QUESTIONS TO *ENERGIZE* YOUR BRAND

No matter what stage of growth you're experiencing, it's important to know the basics of branding and the necessary tools to help you visu-alize your brand. I have had the privilege of working with Samantha Hartley, founder of Enlightened Marketing, on several occasions. Samantha spent years working in Europe, Asia, and the global headquarters for the Coca-Cola Company. When you're associated with building a brand that's now valued at $32 billion, that's impressive. Since her time with Coca-Cola, Samantha has developed over 50 brands for growth companies, nonprofits, and government.

The following excerpts from my interview with Samantha answer nine questions you need to ask about branding. They also eliminate a lot of the urban mythology surrounding branding.

Lisa: *Give us your definition of a brand.*

Samantha: In short, a brand is your unique identity. To expand, you could say that unique identity is a set of attributes and expectations that are associated with you.

Lisa: *Some people believe branding is only important for business-to-consumer firms and irrelevant for business-to-business (B2B). What do you think?*

Samantha: That argument is based on the misconception that branding is all about fancy logos, snappy taglines, and talking lizards. Certainly, none of those elements are going to help your sales team persuade an economic buyer to award you a $20 million contract. However, if your sales team has trouble answering prospective clients' questions like "Why should we hire you for this project?" and "Why are you 30 percent more expensive than the alternatives?" you may benefit from branding and the clarity of message it brings.

Lisa: *What's the difference between a marketing strategy and a brand strategy?*

Samantha: A *marketing strategy* outlines how you intend to attract clients to your business. For B2B companies, this is a defined series of steps to establish your credibility so that, over time, they will eventually want to work with you. This can happen in a few weeks, or it may take years. Once they become clients, it outlines how you will stay in touch with and engage them as they repurchase from you. Marketing strategies are broad initiatives that are broken down into a series of tactics that are usually documented in a marketing plan. Depending on your industry, you might choose marketing strategies like conducting ad campaigns, sending direct mail, publishing white papers, keynote speaking, and exhibiting at trade shows.

Brand strategies can be similar, but the overarching intention of them is to teach your target market who you are, over time, by communicating your brand value in the message. Every marketing message you send—through your statement of values, web site, collateral materials, imagery, dress code, and so on—can build the brand.

Here is an example. If my *marketing strategy* is to reach buyers by exhibiting at regional trade shows, the *brand strategy* is to use all messaging opportunities (booth design, personnel, product demonstrations, giveaways, etc.) to communicate our competitive advantages. You can express your brand through information: the title and topic of a white paper or speech you give suggests your expertise, which is backed up by the demonstrations and messages conveyed by the team in your booth. Valuable information helps to position you as a trusted resource with prospective clients. Candy dishes and cheap trinkets can't compare.

Lisa: *What happens when a company allows the branding process to happen independently from the growth planning process? Or worse yet, it ignores the branding process entirely?*

Samantha: Let's be clear: you'll be branded whether you do this process or not—by your target market, your competitors, and the media. So, growth companies have to slow down long enough to intentionally develop the brand identity they want to be known for.

You don't want to end up like Encyclopedia Britannica, which was almost annihilated by *Wikipedia* and Google. Many once-famous brands took their eyes off the ball long enough for the market or competitors to eradicate them.

As for connecting branding to strategic growth planning, it's important to realize the opportunities created by your brand. The brand is the vehicle for achieving the growth your company is seeking. The marketing team has to know what you want to achieve, then they can design brands and programs that will realize your goals. Disconnected from strategic goals, branding is little more than an expensive academic exercise.

Lisa: *I always thought that branding was reserved for big companies. How can entrepreneurial growth companies build a business case for branding?*

Samantha: If you're trying to sell your organization on branding, there are at least six big benefits. When you have a clear, compelling and authentic brand, with a concise message that everyone in the company can easily express, you'll get.

Benefit 1: A Shorter Sales Cycle

So much of the sales cycle is consumed by the burden of explaining who you are, what you do, and why you're the best choice. Well-branded companies that are marketing to their target audiences consistently will benefit from some awareness of your brand's value, at least, and often from a familiarity with or expectation of benefits.

This can work even with very small businesses. A real estate team I worked with found their distinctive brand imagery was so recognizable that their prospects felt they were "everywhere." Instead of relying on a series of "pitch meetings," they started to sign on new clients in the first meeting.

Benefit 2: A Lower Cost of Client Acquisition

If your sales cycle is shorter, your marketing costs per customer are reduced. When you have a precise brand message, which is laser beamed to your target audience, they don't need to hear it as many times. They don't need to try to figure out what you're telling them. They get it more quickly and understand that it is a good choice, and specifically intended *for them.*

Benefit 3: You Attract Perfect Clients

Many growth businesses are seduced into working with everyone. They try to get good results while working with the wrong clients. They're trying to meet the needs of everyone they can, rather than focusing on those they are best suited to serve. When you're branded well, you attract exactly the right clients for your business: those who have problems you can solve, who are willing to admit they have those problems, and are looking for exactly what you're offering. You can even focus your marketing on those who'll respect your team more, and turn down clients or customers that don't fulfill their agreements. Perfect clients are more profitable, take up a lot less time, and are generally a joy to work with.

Benefit 4: Your Brand Can Carry a Premium Price

When you have a clear message, you can substantiate why you're more expensive and why you're worth it. Few people challenge McKinsey's consulting fees—and they probably never will.

When CEOs of professional services firms complain about the caliber of their clients, I suggest it's time to raise their prices. Rather than destroying their chances at new business, these very skilled companies find that a higher price point actually gets them taken seriously by those who are a much better fit for their services.

Benefit 5: Brand Loyalty Creates Repeat Business

When clear brand messages attract perfect clients, the working relationship almost always goes well. Making a promise about what to expect, and then delivering on it, creates deep satisfaction and loyalty. Your perfect clients will return to you again and again because you've promised—and proven—you're a great fit for them.

Benefit 6: Referrals Flow More Easily

Imagine how excited your perfect, satisfied clients are. They want to share that with their colleagues and friends. We know most people associate with others like themselves, so they'll likely be perfect clients for you as well. A good brand makes it easy for your raving fans to refer you because you have a tightly packaged and differentiated message.

Lisa: *I'm amazed by how many brand touch points truly exist. Which ones do most companies neglect when branding?*

Samantha: I find the least noticeable assets and the lowest paid employees can get forgotten in the branding process. A dirty delivery truck, which is basically a billboard for your brand, can undermine your message even while you're spending thousands of dollars in advertising. A receptionist with lots of regular client contact but no information about your marketing message can claim ignorance when someone asks her about your company. These spoiled or missed opportunities can easily be remedied by briefing everyone who works for or is associated with your brand on the key messages.

Lisa: *You take a different perspective when developing the unique selling proposition (USP) for your clients. Can you tell us about that?*

Samantha: Some of my industry colleagues use a brand discovery process that insists on naming a single differentiator for the brand.

My issue with using this approach for growth companies is the difficulty of finding a single aspect of the brand that differentiates it from all others. While GE may be known for ingenuity, Mercedes-Benz for German engineering and Levi's for ruggedness, it's nearly impossible for a consultant, a community bank, or an architectural firm to find a single, meaningful differentiator that sets it apart from all the rest.

Instead, I use a "portfolio of benefits" approach. I look for two to three things that, when combined or standing alone, can distinguish this brand as truly unique and the superior choice for its target market.

I'll give you an example. I worked with a medical laboratory whose competitors are other private, university, and hospital laboratories. They'd never done any branding before. They had some great points of difference and very unique qualities about them, but they weren't communicating that. They got business through trade shows and word-of-mouth.

What was unique about them? The first thing was that they had pioneered their process with special technology that enabled them to deliver results very quickly. While most of their competitors take up to two weeks to get test results back to patients, this company could *guarantee* delivery within just 48 hours. They had a big point of difference in that.

However, this is a tenuous benefit to base their brand on because it's probable that, eventually, a competitor will figure out how to replicate their speed. That's why I recommended they emphasize other key benefits their loyal clients appreciated: triple quality assurance (three doctors reviewed every test result for accuracy) and a third thing they called the "human factor."

If patients have questions about their test results, they may have only a short amount of time with their own doctors, and it would be nearly impossible to speak with the specialist in the hospital laboratory who analyzed their tests. This company, by contrast, is very accessible for discussion of the results. They were kind and caring on the phone. They demonstrated the human factor.

Let me tell you about the combination of those three things. Nobody would have hired this lab because the doctor was nice and would spend time discussing results with patients. Few would come to this lab just because there was triple quality assurance.

It's their speed that gets new clients in the door. The triple-quality assurance makes people feel good, logically, about the decision they've made. And the human factor gets them referrals.

That's an example of how you can take three dimensions of a brand, any one of which may not be unique, but when combined, makes a company very competitive.

Lisa: *In summary, what are the essential steps to building our brand so that it aligns with our company's growth plan?*

Samantha: The seven-step process I use gets us from big picture of "What do we want to be known for?" all the way down to "What does my sales manager's voice mail message say?"

But first, Lisa, I want to stipulate that this is not a Do-It-Yourself exercise. This is a process in which you need objectivity and insight from an external observer.

I remind my clients who are stuck trying to find their unique identity that "it's hard to read the label from inside the bottle." If you belong to an executive advisory board, ask them to work with you. Or hire a consultant or an agency.

Here are the steps Samantha uses to discover a brand.

Steps to Discover a Brand

1. *Develop a vision of where your business is going, and the role your brand will play in getting it there.* If you can describe what success will look like, it'll be a lot easier to build a road to get there. Draw from what you have developed in step six of your *Energize* Growth® Plan. In other words, describe what your business will look like when it has become the business of your dreams. Include all the ways your business makes money, and what your clients, competitors, and marketplace look like.

The vision statement is a one-page summary document describing, in vivid imagery and motivating language, your business at a future state of success. Write it in present tense from that future point, as if you've already achieved it all.

If you're a growth company, create a vision that extends 18 to 36 months out. A 10-year horizon is too unwieldy.

The vision statement for a city whose brand Samantha helped to update began, "There is a sense of focused energy in Conway—everyone moving on a common path toward similar goals for our city."

This technique may seem New Age, but it actually came from Samantha's days at the Coca-Cola Company. In addition to the vision statement, their business plan one year even included a mock-up of the local paper (in Moscow, Russia) dated three years hence with a headline proclaiming their achievements. This technique unified the team and helped them visualize success.

Remember: The brand is the vehicle that makes your *Energize*Growth® Plan come to life.

2. *Assess the alternatives to your brand.* What is the competitive landscape like, and how do you compare? If prospects don't decide to work with you, who or what might they choose? How often do they choose to do nothing at all? How are you different from those alternatives? Stronger? Weaker?

Knowing that we can't help everyone—and shouldn't—Samantha always likes to explore the reasons the alternatives are more suitable for some than for her perfect clients. Several of my banking clients have come to realize that younger customers would rather have banking on their mobile phones than a warm, personal relationship with a banker. If their strength is in warmth but not in technology, they will struggle to attract this type of customer.

For many technology or professional services firms, the biggest "competitors" end up being the client doing it themselves or deciding to do nothing. If this is the case, rather than spending time saying why you're the best of all the service providers, you really must communicate why a company would benefit from working with you rather than by doing it themselves.

3. *Define your target market.* Exactly who needs what you offer and will most value how it helps them? Again, this is a key element you have gleaned from building your *Energize*Growth® Plan. Samantha tries to clone her current, most perfect client by getting specific about what makes them such a good fit for her brand, then recall how they found her (through which marketing channel), what persuaded them to work with her, and then extrapolate: where can she find more just like them?

4. *Isolate your specific point of difference or USP.* We discussed the portfolio of benefits earlier and how they combine to set you apart from all the alternatives. Your differentiation can be the beneficial solution you offer, how you offer it, or whom you offer it to. Whatever

you choose, it must be clear, compelling, authentic, and consistently communicated.

It's critical to collect and incorporate feedback from your target market about what *they* believe to be your differentiation. Ideally, the greater part of that market research should come from raving fans. They are clients who "get" your brand value more than anyone. Your raving fans will be able to tell you what they find so valuable, and then you can decide if that's what you want your brand to stand for.

5. *Standardize the language of your brand with positioning statements and elevator statements, and develop your brand's look and feel.* Ultimately, all your work on the brand must reduce to a concise, persuasive statement that everyone in your company, as well as your referral partners, can recite. Here is an example: "ABC Tutoring works with high school students [target market] who stress out when taking tests [problem or need]. We blend proven scientific approaches with nontraditional techniques like meditation and EFT to help improve scores by up to 40 percent [differentiation and proof]."

In addition, develop a distinctive and memorable look and feel for your brand that includes a logo to represent it, color scheme, and visual style, imagery, and a "voice" to use in your marketing communications.

6. *Select the marketing strategies you'll use to deliver the message of your brand to your target market.* As we mentioned earlier, effective ways to emanate your message may include writing articles, developing online communities of raving fans, or speaking on signature topics. Networking is a short-term yet effective strategy for delivering your message face-to-face. Be sure your client or brand surveys ask your target market the best way for you to stay connected with them.

7. *Cascade the brand through all touch points.* What does consistency in brand message delivery look like? It's when every "touch"

you have with your customers builds on the previous messages you have conveyed. This results in an ever more robust experience.

Determine how you could best communicate your brand message through each brand touch point. For instance, if one of your differentiators is efficiency, you might return calls within two hours, include a value statement about efficiency on your business card, and strive to provide instant messaging and auto-responder tools through your web site that help your clients increase their efficiency.

Lisa: *What reactions should CEOs expect when their brand becomes crystal clear?*

Samantha: Elation, relief, and a renewed pride and enthusiasm for the company are very common. It's kind of like falling in love all over again because you are reminded just what was so great about this company in the first place.

I've had people gasp during meetings when the right thing was said in just the right way. They've had teams of people out there improvising for years, trying to find exactly the right phrase, and then in the midst of this arduous creative process, a phrase comes up and captures the essence beautifully.

When your brand is clear and you're spreading the message consistently, you will have an energized staff, interested prospects, and a thriving business.

BRANDING IN ACTION

Whether you lead a rapidly growing million-dollar services firm or a mature, well-established $14 billion bank, the need for branding is just as critical. Let's look at how two companies on different ends of the size spectrum are doing this effectively.

Shawn Solloway, president of EXIT Marketing, was bitten by the startup bug in 2003. He saw a great need to build a company that was focused on helping clients whose messages were getting lost in the advertising clutter. Today, EXIT Marketing's mission is simple: to end bad advertising.

Solloway saw an untapped market opportunity. He observed that during the creative development stage, many advertising agencies focused very few resources on refining their clients' messaging so that it was truly engaging. Unlike other agencies, EXIT offers a level of creativity that cuts through the tremendous ad clutter and engages customers. Doing this gets clients greater results faster. Emotionally engaging messages are remembered more easily. People remember what they feel. Through doing this, less media spending is required to get desired results.

EXIT Marketing's focus on developing their own brand has paid great dividends. Just five years after founding the company, Solloway has enjoyed 40 percent revenue growth and has expanded to seven professionals (S. Solloway, personal communication, September 12 2008).

Even well-established banks can teach us something about branding. Umpqua Bank demonstrates that creativity and innovation can even energize companies who are entrenched in notoriously conservative industries. Compared to the other bank CEOs that our team interviewed in 2007, Umpqua Bank's Ray Davis was one of a handful who wasn't ashamed to use the term *marketing.* His current book, *Leading for Growth,* outlines his secrets to success.

When it comes to branding and strategy, Davis says:

> I get most of my ideas from companies that have nothing to do with banking. But most of my competitors in the banking industry, bless 'em, don't try to learn from other industries. . . . You could walk into a Gap store and know that's where you were even if you didn't see the signs. Same with Banana Republic, Victoria's Secret, and so on. These were revolutions that were obvious in retail. But my industry slept on. Every bank you walked into was the

same as every other. They all came in one flavor: plain vanilla (Davis 2007, 142).

In 1995, Umpqua Bank invented the "bank store" concept. Instead of comparing themselves to *banking leaders,* Davis reached out and benchmarked their brand against *brand leaders* such as Starbucks and Hewlett-Packard. They even brew their own blend of coffee for customers who stop by their stores.

Davis' relentless commitment to linking marketing strategy and branding with execution has paid off. Umpqua Bank was selected by *BusinessWeek* as one of the most original ideas of 2005. And in spite of the banking industry downturn in 2008, their stock traded at a 25 to 40 percent premium compared to other community banks (Google Finance n.d.). You will find brand inspiration in many places, often from industries unrelated to your own. Now that you have looked at your *Energize* Growth® Plan and your brand from *outside* the bottle, it is safe to remove the warning label.

Energy Booster 9

What is our brand promise—and how can we fulfill that promise even more consistently?

CHAPTER 10

More Revenues, Fewer Clients

We never know the worth of water 'til the well is dry.
—ENGLISH PROVERB

The sweet taste of success is driven by how effectively you implement your plan and manage your mindset. Now let's examine how your perception of value shapes your pricing strategies.

For most creatures, behaviors are rather predictable. Our three cats remind us of this universal truth. In our home, our cats Picard, Fisan, and Big B rule the roost. It never ceases to amaze me how much they love routine—and to what extremes they will go to ensure their routines are not disrupted.

Their day begins with organic, overpriced canned food. They howl if we don't give them a mid-morning treat. In the evening, we tuck them into "purgatory"—their makeshift bedroom that doubles as the laundry room.

Our cats won't challenge the status quo. And who can blame them for savoring their 24-hour concierge service?

Since the dawn of the Industrial Age, many humans have become attached to another pattern: the method by which we communicate and deliver value, and how we price our services accordingly. Depending on our perspective, they can either be extremely empowering or severely limiting.

Let's look first at how we position our value in the market by distinguishing between fees and value. According to Alan Weiss, author of *Value Based Fees: How to Charge—and Get—What You're Worth,* "fees are dependent on value provided in the perception of the buyer and on the intent of the buyer and the services provider to do the right thing—to act ethically" (Weiss 2002, 3).

In other words, value is a byproduct of several factors: the perception of your brand, your ability to communicate your brand clearly and ethically, and how consistently your brand and delivery mechanisms align to ultimately create a wonderful client experience. For all you left-brained readers, this will drive you somewhat crazy. There is an art to creating value, and it cannot always be quantified. It takes a blend of great listening skills, the ability to think on your feet, and the courage to be provocative. If you are not willing to challenge and provoke your prospects and clients, you are probably in the wrong profession. You may be better suited to be a full-time employee who takes guidance and direction from a leadership team. This is not a judgment statement. True trusted advisors are unafraid to be unpopular in order to be catalysts for inspiration and change.

Just ask Zipcar about creating value. This company has turned the car rental industry on its head. Zipcar calls themselves a "car sharing" company. Instead of renting a car by visiting a rental counter, filling out miles of paperwork, and paying steep rates and surcharges, you use their online and onsite self-service approach. You can join Zipcar online, check rates in your targeted city, and rent by the hour or day. You can select from a wide variety of styles, makes, and models. By swiping your Zipcar membership card on the windshield, the car unlocks. You can even purchase a car if you wish. Since they were founded in 2000, they have added 200,000 customers to their online database. They now operate in 25 U.S. cities and London. They bond people to car rentals by involving people emotionally in the rental process and giving each car a unique nickname. Who ever thought that a company could reawaken a sleepy industry by redefining value through instant, affordable mobility?

Delivering value has become ever so important in today's business world. Value delivery has become a rather recent phenomenon in the world of commerce.

Looking back in time, hunter-gatherer societies did not need to worry about delivering value. They just worried about basic safety, food, and shelter for their tribes. It wasn't until agrarian, or farming societies emerged that specialization and currency began to play a role in maintaining and growing societies. Barter was still popular, and the idea of assigning proper value of a pig in exchange for live produce began to emerge.

During the turn of the nineteenth century, the Agrarian Age gave rise to the Industrial Age. This was a significant turn of events in our history. Much like the guilds of medieval times, labor unions became strong, and ensured that fair wages and working conditions were in place. The focus of businesses was on mass production, maximizing profits, and managing things.

The birth of mainframe and minicomputers drove the dawn of the Information Age around 1970. It spawned many new industries around controlling and providing information. In fact, I worked for one of the first personal computer software companies in the early 1980s—a job that did not even exist while I attended college. Clients and investors placed value in the talents of computer programmers, systems designers, database architects, software engineers, and hardware jockeys. It was a great time to be part of this burgeoning industry.

The Information Age began morphing in the 1980s. Companies across multiple industries began focusing not just on what benefits they delivered, but on the *complete* customer experience. Once people had products, they wanted service to go along with it. Now that service is expected, they want everything else surrounding products or services—all of the various *experiences* of working with your company—to meet their expectations. Astute companies that understand that service is no longer the differentiator it once was have expanded their focus to the whole experience, and they have prospered from their insight. Just look at how Starbucks transformed itself in the 1990s. They shifted from being viewed as a chain of 350 premium coffee stores to a meeting place that was known as "Rewarding Everyday Moments."

Most companies have now shifted from placing a value on *things* and *information* to placing great value on *knowledge*. The Knowledge Age, which is a term that Peter Drucker and Stephen Covey often used, is more about finding your voice, and inspiring others to find theirs. The focus is no longer on managing things; it's on leading people.

It is paramount that we understand the paradigms and trends that are driving this new era in order to understand our contribution to it. Says Covey:

> Do you believe that the Information/Knowledge Worker Age we're moving into will out produce the Industrial Age fifty times? I believe it will. We're just barely beginning to see it. . . . Nathan Myhrvold, former Chief Technology Officer of Microsoft, put it this way: "The top software developers are more productive than average software developers not by a factor of 10X or 100X or even 1000X, but by a factor of 10,000X." Quality knowledge work is so valuable that unleashing its potential offers organizations an extraordinary opportunity for value creation (Covey 2004, 14).

True business success is grounded in people, and how well we treat them—within and outside our World Wide Web.

Memorizing this brief economics history lesson is not important. If you forget everything else so far, remember just one thing: *In the business world, our Industrial Age point of view still believes that time spent on a task equates to value.* That belief perpetuates hourly billing structures. Conversely, the Knowledge Age point of view believes that value equates to the experience, education, and inspiration that we provide to others, and subsequently helps them find their own voice. If that takes five months versus five hours, the value is still the same.

Therein lies the dissonance. *Although we are living in a new age, our mindsets around value have gotten stuck in a time warp!*

Education and pedigree seem to have little impact on our ability to break free from this antiquated point of view. Just look at how most law firms operate. The hourly rate for a newly qualified lawyer at a big firm in the United States or the United Kingdom can reach $500. Many firms even set billable hour targets for their lawyers. These can exceed 1,800 hours. Worse than that, lawyers who exceed their targets often get a bonus. Some clients are in an uproar because they believe this encourages padding. Thankfully, companies such as Eversheds are changing this antiquated business practice.

Eversheds: Shedding the Old Ways of Doing Business

One global law firm has bucked the "hours for dollars" trend successfully and challenged the implicit conflict of interest in the legal profession. Eversheds, an international business law firm headquartered in the United Kingdom, is unique in its industry because they are known for delivering consistent service across 25 countries and 40 cities. Ten years ago, their clients expressed a need for a more sophisticated approach to rewarding their law firms.

According to Stephen Hopkins, partner and head of international integration, "Our clients felt a lack of control over the legal spend, a lack of transparency over how the spend was amassed, and a need to align the billing to the goals of the business itself. Law firms have a poor reputation when it comes

(continued)

(Continued)

to billing. If you measure or bill by the hour, then the behavior you get is to encourage the recording of more and more hours."

Eversheds penned an agreement with Tyco in 2007 to handle their commercial legal work across Europe, the Middle East, and Africa for a fixed fee. Tyco used to work with 282 firms. Now they work exclusively with Eversheds in Europe, the Middle East, and Africa. Hopkins explains that:

> Prior to beginning any legal work, Eversheds' team is required to provide an estimate for that particular matter into their Global Account Management System. Nobody is allowed to start any work until they complete that form. We check it in the U.K., and send it to the relevant client/decision maker for approval. The client either accepts the estimate, requests further information, chooses to do the project in house, or challenges the estimate. We never bill above that estimate. Any revisions to the estimates require prior client approval.

When it comes to pricing litigation-related services, Eversheds withholds 10 percent of its fees. Hopkins continues:

> If our firm meets the goals we agreed to with the client, we bill another 10 percent. If we do not, we get only 90 percent of our fees. If we exceed the business objectives, we get 125 percent of the fees. We are working with Tyco on ways to reduce or avoid litigation. We will get a bonus if we can either reduce the number of lawsuits brought against Tyco or if we can reduce the number of lawsuits that Tyco issues by 15 percent. The cost saving

to Tyco more than compensates for the bonus we are paid.

Their client has already reaped the rewards. This new pricing model has helped reduce the Tyco legal spend by 20 to 25 percent. Hopkins estimates that this equates to at least a $2 million savings.

Source: S. Hopkins, personal communication, October 13, 2008.

I encourage every company who is trapped in the "hours for dollars" paradigm to escape now. And if you work with any hourly based service providers, ask them for a value-driven fee structure if they want to keep you as a client.

Whether I'm working with a technology firm, high-end resort, or a business advisory firm, I see the same dissonance in how they communicate their value. This causes too many companies to be paid much less than what they're worth. This keeps them on the hourly rate treadmill. Here are the reasons why these Industrial Age mindsets linger:

- *They don't do their homework.* I am shocked at how many times the members of my action groups completely improvise before an important client discovery/exploratory call. They come across unprofessional and unprepared.

- *They forget that perceived value and the quality of the relationship are the basis of the fee, not the hours worked.* They consequently focus their time on lowering the fees instead of managing the value.

- *They do not translate the importance of their advice or offer into the long-term benefits and gains as perceived by the client.* Instead, they think they must base their value on deliverables, not measurable outcomes. These deliverables may be a design consultation, a workshop, a series of manager interviews, online assessments, or a coaching session. In reality, these are commodities. If you don't believe me, use your web browser to search for "sales training." See if you can differentiate between the 27 million search hits.

- *They fail to develop a relationship with the economic buyer.* An economic buyer must fulfill several key characteristics: they can either write the check or order the check to be written for your services and they establish priorities for their organization. Without this economic buyer relationship, "the client may not do the right thing ethically (delay payment, argue about your value, arbitrarily change objectives)" (Weiss 2002, 3).

- *They lack the confidence or belief that they really can deliver a high level of value to their client.* The fees reach a level that equates to your level of self-worth. Could Weiss be right when he says that consultants—not clients—are the main cause of low consulting fees?

Mindsets around value can make or break your business growth. Consider these factors as you navigate the various stages of growth we discussed in Chapter 7. Ask yourself whether your own personal definition of value might be the biggest wall you need to scale.

How can we make hourly rates the mark of a bygone era, once and for all?

Dumping hourly rates is all about reaching agreement with clients on value. If, for instance, you propose to help a client reduce employee attrition rates by 20 percent, then you must quantify that cost reduction and suggest ways to measure it.

According to Michael McLaughlin of RainToday.com, a prominent online community and publication for consultants, "Some consultants argue that it's too difficult to quantify the value of a consulting project in advance. But those who take the time to nail

TABLE 10.1   Drivers of Consulting Value

Increase	Reduce	Improve	Create
Revenue	Costs	Productivity	Strategy
Profit	Time/effort	Processes	Systems
Growth	Complaints	Service	Processes
Value	Risk	Information	Business
Retention	Turnover	Morale	Products
ROI or ROA	Conflict	Reputation	Services
Efficiency	Paperwork	Skills	Brand
Visibility		Loyalty	
		Quality	

Source: Michael McLaughlin, RainToday. Reprinted with permission.

down that value will encounter less price resistance from clients, especially if the value-to-fee ratio is high" (McLaughlin 2004).

Some values will be easier to measure than others. It is important to engage your clients in a frank discussion of what your services are worth. This is a key phase in your sales conversation with a prospective client. Your job is to ask the engaging questions to uncover the possible drivers of value for your products and services. McLaughlin provides some great examples in Table 10.1—and they do not just apply to consulting firms.

Once you have articulated project benefits with your client, it is up to you to estimate what the proposed changes are worth.

You might help clients improve the quality of their products, which should result in fewer complaints and returns and lower inventory carrying costs. If you improve morale among a client's staff, managers could spend less time micro-managing minutiae and more time running the business. Given the average cost of replacing a good employee can be 150 percent of their annual salary (or more), this can be an attractive return on investment.

Quantify all benefits that are relevant to a project, and confirm those numbers with the client in writing. Weiss (2002, 11) considers this to be a key part of what he calls the "conceptual agreement." This agreement must clearly describe three things:

1. The key *objectives* for the engagement (What improvements or new ways of operating does the client want to attain?)

2. The *value* to the client (How will your client be better off—financially, emotionally, or otherwise—when they meet those objectives?)

3. The *measures of success* (How will the client measure improvement? How will they track the success of working with your firm?)

A conceptual agreement provides the crucial context for you and your client to assess the true value of what you offer and becomes the centerpiece to establishing your fees.

Once you've agreed with the client on value, you can use any number of pricing methods. You have many from which to choose, including contingency billing (popular with executive recruiters), fixed fees, success fees (well accepted by consultants who sell services to startups), partial success fees, and value-based billing. Most importantly, you'll be in a position to kiss that Industrial Age thinking goodbye.

DEMONSTRATE YOUR VALUE NOW: 16 WAYS TO GENERATE MORE REVENUES FROM FEWER CLIENTS

Now that you understand the outdated approaches to defining value, take some proactive measures to keep them at bay:

1. *Convince yourself that you're worth it.* This is the toughest step, and the first wall you have to scale. Start by listening to how you communicate your value. Eliminate words such as *hourly* or *daily fees* from your vocabulary and your web site. Write down at least five

statements and post them in your office that will remind you of the value you deliver. For example, in my office, I keep a list of three or four success stories near the phone. When a prospect asks me what I have done for other clients, I can readily describe a client who faced a similar situation within just 20 to 30 seconds. The more I practice these stories, the more confident I feel about our firm's fees. In the past year, not one prospective client has questioned our fees.

2. *Consider raising prices annually by at least 10 percent.* This helps you weed out the bottom feeder clients, maintain strong cash flow, and keep pace with the increased value your company should deliver over time.

Ask yourself some key questions before you announce the price increase. For example, when was the last time you actually demonstrated and communicated the level of value that you actually deliver? Any sound trusted advisor schedules regular status meetings with the economic buyer to review progress, make mid-course corrections, and celebrate any wins.

Make a list of all variables that may justify the need for a price increase. Here are some to consider:

- *Elapsed time since your last price increase:* If you have not increased prices for 15 months or more, then it's time for an increase.

- *Your niche has changed:* Have you recently become more specialized? Is your solution becoming well known within a specific region or industry? Your ongoing focus on a certain market or demographic will warrant higher fees.

- *Break-even point on your offerings:* Be sure to strike a balance between what you *need* to make versus what you *want* to make.

- *Cost of traveling to/from client locations.*

- *All forms of insurance:* Include liability, health, automobile, and Errors and Omissions (E&O).

- *Technology costs:* Include web hosting, hardware, software, network support, and security systems.

- *Local and regional market conditions:* What is your market willing to pay? One of the reasons our team continues to work in 20 countries is that our local market generally pays very low fees for strategy consulting. Unfortunately, many local consultants are semi-retired. They are less interested in expanding their practice and more interested in leisure time. As a result, they have conditioned the few companies who can afford to hire consultants that hourly rates and "pay-as-you-go" training days are acceptable payment methods.

- *New certifications and professional development programs:* These support your efforts to stay competitive and create more value for your clients.

- *Positioning against your competitors or alternative solutions:* Are you viewed as the "crème de la crème" in your field, or a low-cost body shop for hire? Identifying your niche and positioning makes pricing decisions much easier. If you are unaware of what your competitors are charging, try posting inquiries on various industry forums. Develop a proprietary study that you can sell back to your clients to help them evaluate future service providers and offerings. Or hire an independent consultant to conduct some research and purchase the report from them. A simple posting on Google Answers, Craigslist, LinkedIn, or elance.com will generate volumes of qualified responses. Just be sure to use an e-mail account that doesn't reflect your company name, such as Gmail or Yahoo!

- *Number of new staff members:* Have you recently expanded your team, or acquired new products and services under your business umbrella? Now is the time to simultaneously announce a price increase. You will find yourself investing in more infrastructure, office space, technology, and support staff to help new hires get up to speed. Your prices must rise accordingly.

Finally, determine the scope of your fee increases. Will you raise your fees across the board, or just for new clients? How much advance notice will you provide your existing clients to apprise them of the increase? What percentage of clients are you willing to kiss goodbye?

3. *Develop a highly professional looking, search engine-optimized web site that offers free valuable stuff.* As your firm becomes more recognized by media and you receive more referrals, people will naturally want to visit your web site. They will not make a purchasing decision based on your site; however, they will use it to determine whether you are truly qualified and credible. They need to experience what you do and how you do it. A web site should contain, at a minimum, the following pages:

- *Descriptive biographies of every key team member:* Not resumes—but descriptions of how each person helps your clients attain measurable results, and what they enjoy doing within and outside the company.

- *A simple, conversational home page that allows the reader to assess mutual fit:* Here is an example from Creative Office Environments: www.creative-va.com. Their web site reflects their company's focus: to develop customized solutions for ergonomics in the workplace that positively impact team productivity and financial performance. Their leading question on their home page is, *Is your work environment inspiring innovation?* Then it leads you toward other pages that explain their client successes and approach. The site is clean, simple, and capable of crossing global language boundaries.

- *A healthy collection of free information that inspires, informs, and educates:* These can include short articles (under 750 words), reprints of articles you've written, short white papers, assessments, surveys, podcasts, MP3 audios, blog postings, short videos, and client success stories. Two web sites are noteworthy in this area: www.hubspot.com and www.pragmaticmarketing.com. They offer endless resources that encourage you to return often. I was so impressed by Hubspot's information that I became a customer.

4. *Develop joint ventures with successful people and top-notch mentors.* Your success is a direct reflection of the expectations of your peers. One of the best connectors of business professionals I have met is Melissa Giovagnoli, author of *Networlding*. She helps professionals build better relationships and close more sales. Crain's recently named Giovagnoli the top networker in Chicago, Illinois.

Giovagnoli suggests you create a "Circle of Ten"—a group of 10 highly reliable, diverse influencers who consistently support your business. According to Giovagnoli, "Our brains are neural networks, our transportation systems are networks, television is a network, and the Internet is the network of all networks. When we embrace network thinking, we are able to really harness the power of the network" (Giovagnoli 2008).

5. *Automate everything you can.* I am amazed at how many multimillion-dollar firms are still operating with antiquated systems. The customer relationship management revolution (and I use that term sarcastically) tried to convince us that automating your sales processes would transform our business and delight our customers. They forgot to tell us that we first needed to have a streamlined, documented sales process before we tried to automate it!

Before you automate any of your business systems, determine which processes are no longer necessary. Determine which processes are done manually—but are highly ineffective. Don't automate a poor process and expect positive results. Sit down and document your core business processes. Then consider these categories, and how you can streamline them:

- Sales.

- Finance: Online merchant accounts, online banking, accounting software, and so on.

- Administration: Travel planning, appointment setting, research, facility maintenance, and so on.

- Marketing activity: Research, lead generation, lead conversion, publicity, public relations, and so on.

- Technical support: Backup and recovery systems, hardware support, software maintenance and support, upgrades, and so on.

- Legal: Copyright protection, trademarks, intellectual property, labor law, workers compensation, safety.

I have found some excellent tools to simplify your business. I have no financial ties to these companies, so I offer no guarantee of their future capabilities or your possible results. Some of my favorites are:

- *Sharing calendars across multiple locations:* www.timebridge.com

- *Managing time zones:* www.timeanddate.com

- *Customer relationship management:* Salesforce.com and Avidian Technologies

- *Capture ideas, business cards, notes, photos, white boards, and "to do" lists:* www.evernote.com

- *Teleconferencing services:* www.freeconferencecall.com and Great American Networks, www.ganconference.com

- *Virtual assistants:* AssistU, www.assistu.com; Your Man in India, www.ymii.com; and Brickwork India, www.b2kcorp.com

- *Web conferencing services:* www.gotomeeting.com

I won't even try to recommend wireless, portable, and handheld tools. By the time this book is printed, they will have been upstaged by newer devices. Suffice it to say that they are essential in this flat world. The list should get you started on your automation journey.

6. *Write scripts to guide your thoughtful, high-value conversations.* Develop questions and discussion guides for several areas of business development. These include:

- *A series of well prepared, open ended questions to explore the prospective client needs:* "Unlock the Game's" Ari Galper has mastered the art of asking nonmanipulative questions to diagnose and prioritize client needs. Visit www.unlockthegame for details. These will also help you identify the true economic buyer.

- *A simple way to propose a possible solution.*

- *Questions for identifying the economic buyer:* Some sources tell me that in our current recession, selling cycles for business-to-business offerings have doubled. What will your strategies be for reaching that person as quickly as possible?

- *A written, one- to two-page marketing plan and process to announce new offerings to existing clients.*

- *A structured way to ask for referrals.* I used to simply ask a friendly business colleague, "If you stumble upon someone who can benefit from our services, please let me know." This is the worst form of requesting referrals. Nobody will ever remember what you're requesting. Consider developing a confidential "referral profile" document. This short document contains snapshots of your elevator statement, unique selling proposition, why people hire your company, ideal client, characteristics of a less than ideal client, when it makes sense for clients to hire you, two or three very short client success stories, how you handle their referrals, and your full contact information. Take 10 minutes and walk your referral sources through this document. Leave a copy for them. They will be glad you did.

7. *Learn how to write professional proposals.* In the first 15 years of my career, over 60 percent of my proposals were rejected, and prospects would literally disappear.

In other cases, I have seen proposals that took hours to read. They include timelines, complex charts, product descriptions, and team biographies. Companies often use them to showcase how smart they are, instead of focusing on the client's objectives and intended outcomes. I found an oasis of wisdom when I encountered *Million Dollar Consulting* by Alan Weiss. He recommends that a proposal contain nine key points:

1. Appraisal of the client's situation

2. Objectives

3. Measures of success

4. Value to the organization

5. Methodology and options

6. Timing

7. Joint accountabilities

8. Terms and conditions (fees, investment options, expiration date, payment plans, prepayment discounts, expenses covered, etc.)

9. Acceptance/signatures (Weiss 2003, 187–191)

8. *Develop relationships primarily with economic buyers.* Even when you think you know who the true buyer is, clients can deceive you. This can be very frustrating. By asking the following questions, your chances of investing time with the right people increase dramatically:

- Who has the most to gain from this project?

- Who has the most to lose if this project is cancelled or fails?

- Which executive will sponsor this engagement?

- Who will report your results and success back to the board of directors?

- Whose budget will support this project?

- Which department or division will be most supportive of this initiative?

- Who in your organization tried to solve this issue in the past, and what were the results?

- Whose bonus and performance will be most affected by the success of this project?

9. *Stop doing favors, such as free speeches and free consulting.* I met with a West Coast advertising firm that was struggling to manage cash flow. The CEO was very well respected in his community and had won several awards from his peers. The CEO allowed new clients to sign on without a written agreement … a handshake would seal the deal, and his team would begin work in hopes of securing payment terms later.

That company's receivables grew to $60,000 in just one month, and they were weeks away from closing their doors. We strongly persuaded him to cut back on his numerous volunteer activities and commitments. He also began developing more formal written agreements with clients. They reduced their receivables by 50 percent within just one month.

If you are really passionate about certain nonprofits, put your extra time, talent, and treasury into those—not doing a bunch of "freebies" for your clients on a regular basis. Great clients are not charity cases, and do not want to be treated as such.

10. *Interview clients regularly to gather and document success stories.* Publish every success story on your web site and several media outlets. Some of my favorites are local community business publications, PRWeb.com, and industry associations where your clients gather.

11. *Work hard at doing things that others cannot do.* During difficult economic times, it pays to stand out. While many of your competitors scale back on growth and marketing, your company can shine. Consider launching a new product or service at a time that your competition is asleep. For example, if your industry normally launches products or services during a certain holiday season, consider launching those two months in advance around a specific industry event—while your competition isn't expecting it.

12. *If appropriate, offer an extraordinary guarantee.* If you want to really differentiate your offering, inspire trust, and remove any perceived risk, consider offering an extraordinary guarantee. This goes a long way toward proving that you can give your prospects exactly what they need. When you do this, you get much closer to tipping the scales toward a sale.

In some cases, an extraordinary guarantee may not work for your line of business. According to Christopher Hart, author of *Extraordinary Guarantees,* it makes sense when:

- Your offerings are high priced (and hence, the client is more risk-averse).

- Your client's image is at risk.

- The negative consequences of service failure are high (backup software, wedding planning).

- Your industry has a bad reputation around service quality. Think about industries such as home security systems, high-end hair stylists, body shops, CRM software, life coaches, and personal injury lawyers.

- Your firm relies heavily on word-of-mouth, especially through the blogosphere, where bad news travels fast.

- Your growth potential relies heavily on repeat business (Hart 1988, 59).

Some companies may only need to offer conditional guarantees to grow client confidence. When I lead action groups for my small business clients, I publish the program guarantee on the welcome page. I guarantee a partial refund to any client when one or more of these conditions apply:

- The client is not completely satisfied.

- Client's business closes.

- Company is acquired.

- Family illness or emergency.

- If they participate in eight out of the nine sessions, complete the homework assignments, and still do not experience any results.

In early 2007, JetBlue Airways launched a very creative guarantee in response to a series of bad customer service events. Some passengers were stranded on the tarmac for up to 11 hours. Within just days of this customer service breakdown, they announced a "Passenger Bill of Rights." CEO David Neeleman presented discounted or free flight options if customers' flights were delayed by more than one hour, and increased staffing to handle future emergencies. Was this extraordinary? You bet. Analysts are slowly upgrading the stock, and JetBlue is aggressively undergoing modernization activity in their main terminals.

13. *Develop and nurture trusting relationships.* Create a list of A clients and find ways to delight them. Send them a book or an article they may find useful. Invite them to lunch as a way of saying "I appreciate you." Support their pet projects and nonprofit ventures. This list may be just 10 economic buyers. It may be 100. The number is not as important as the quality of the connection. According to Alan Weiss:

> Value is not only created by scarcity. It is created by the worth of the relationship. Trusting relationships with

buyers create higher fees. The longer you take to develop strong relationships, the faster you are able to create high-worth and high-fee projects. . . . I may offer the same services as larger firms, but I beat the competition every time because I'm able to generate a much more trusting relationship with the buyer (Weiss 2006).

14. *Schedule celebrations to honor your clients, partners, and suppliers.* Last summer, I hosted a special outdoor retreat and luncheon. I invited two groups: my clients and members of my dream team—namely, the vendors, suppliers, and referral partners who made me look good. The intention of the event was threefold: to publicly recognize my dream team, refer them more business, and help my current clients find prescreened, proven resources with less effort.

The results exceeded my expectations. Not only did my clients save several weeks' worth of time screening and hiring great service providers—they started doing more business with each other. They formed joint ventures and reached new levels of trust. They naturally are raving fans for *Energize*Growth®. This has become an annual event.

15. *Walk in your client's shoes.* Your company may offer a great product or service, but some aspect of the experience might be sending your ideal clients to competitors. Every person in your organization should periodically field inbound calls, resolve a client problem, or assist with a service call.

16. *Give your CFO a seat at the value production table.* If you are into the growth stage or at a second brick wall, accountability becomes essential. What better person to help you with this discipline than your financial officer? When our team worked with Mark Pollock, CFO of Avanceon, we were pleased to see how Pollock took the role of accountability expert seriously. Their company is dependent on payments that tie directly to meeting certain project milestones. Systems integrators are notorious for facing cash flow issues because clients frequently request change orders. He began attending team

project status meetings to improve his own project visibility. In one instance, Avanceon's team had delivered on schedule and expected a $50,000 milestone payment upon client testing—but the client wanted to delay the testing phase. Pollock asked the account team to amend the client agreement, which they did successfully. As a result, the client paid on schedule. And within just a few months, the company saw its days sales outstanding (DSO) decline from 70 days to 45 days.

Creating and sustaining value isn't the only thing that will energize your business growth. It's *everything.*

Don't be a creature of habit (like our cats). Select just two of these tips to implement immediately, and watch how your Wealth Quotient increases.

Energy Booster 10

What can we do immediately to expand our perception of our value and attract clients who will pay us commensurate with that value?

CHAPTER 11

Future Energy Sources: How to Grow Your Wealth Quotient with Social Media

The power of the press, satellite, and wireless networks resides in the hands of everyone with access to the Internet. Traditional media and publishing will never be the same again. That's empowering and maddening at the same time. Without a clear understanding of that shift in power and influence, we can sabotage our growth and damage relationships.

Social media defines a category of Web-based tools that facilitate information sharing. Much of its attraction is attributed to the freedom and flexibility associated with user-generated content. These typically include blogs, online videos, and social networks. You can find thousands of networking sites where social media makers gather. Among business-to-business (B2B) companies, LinkedIn, Zing, Twitter, and Plaxo (now a Comcast subsidiary) are highly popular networking venues. In the online retail sector, the largest social networks used are Facebook, MySpace, and YouTube ("Consumers Await on Social Networks" 2008). Twitter is rapidly climbing the market acceptance ladder. You can either join a current network, or use portals such as www.ning.com to create your own social network.

The Technology Adoption Life Cycle, which was made famous by Geoffrey Moore in *Crossing the Chasm,* gives us an idea on how widely accepted social media have become and how many people consider them to be viable business strategies. Such disruptive innovations—which are defined as those products and services that have the ability to dramatically alter the competitive landscape—go through similar phases in technology adoption. Some forms of social media and networking sites are as much a discontinuous innovation as the Apple iPhone, ZipCar, and virtual office assistants.

In the business arena, social media acceptance is happening at a slower pace than in the personal arena. That's because many executives find that networking sites cannot (yet) prove a solid return on their investment. In other words, they have not crossed the chasm and achieved widespread market acceptance and adoption.

According to Mark Cavender, managing director of Chasm Institute LLC:

> Consumer examples of disruptive social media include Twitter, which relies on the notion that people really do care what you are doing at a particular time, and Digg, which relies on "wisdom of the crowds." Yet other forms of consumer social media are not that disruptive. Like eBay, they take an activity that has been largely event- (or temporal) and location-driven and turn it into something that is now process-driven, not restricted to time or place. The social media category on the consumer side, namely Facebook, Twitter, and MySpace, is on Main Street as far as adoption by young people ages 12 to 29. But from a business monetization standpoint, they are either in the Chasm or just crossing it.

> On the business side, LinkedIn has made its way solidly into the Bowling Alley. Those who have it cannot imagine life without it. It is also making its way in monetization. They recently closed a "D" round of financing including their original investors. Professionals like LinkedIn because it offers real utility to those seeking to network, post or seek jobs, keep in touch with former colleagues, etc.

Their user base is very different from MySpace, Facebook (for individuals) and the rest in that they are more affluent and willing to pay for these benefits. Zing and Facebook are also worthy alternatives in business but have yet to cross the monetization chasm. While there is no clear gorilla (or strong market leader) yet, which is what ultimately happens in a Tornado market, the winds appear to be blowing in LinkedIn's direction for business adoption. Individuals and businesspeople grow weary of having so many alternatives, and the market simply cannot and will not support many generic sites. (M. Cavender, personal communication, October 24, 2008)

Think about your own company's response—or sense of overwhelm—when it comes to social media. How many different social networks, blogs, forums, online newsletters, and new media outlets have you been asked to join? Notice how long it takes to set up a profile that truly reflects your company brand and vision. This process alone can be a full-time job, and a questionable use of your time. That's why many of us just can't imagine maintaining multiple sites and profiles.

The attraction to social media, however, is undeniable. People who are passionate about their business love to connect with other like-minded individuals, and they will often invest the time to establish these profiles and networks. Social networks in particular provide that vehicle. Sometimes, these networks can yield great rewards. As you'll learn in this chapter, one company has secured an alliance agreement valued in the millions through LinkedIn. In other cases, these outlets can destroy your brand and growth ambitions overnight.

In 2007, the chairman and CEO of a public company saw his company's Wealth Quotient (WQ) decline precipitously within just a few months.

It all started when he created a bogus, anonymous online account within Yahoo's online financial community. Then, over an eight-year period, he anonymously posted glowing comments about his company. Journalists soon wrote a breaking news story about his trail of over 1,400 postings. Some people accused him of intentionally deriding his main competitor so that he could deflate their stock price and make a pending acquisition with their main competitor more favorable to the CEO's company. His activities soon triggered a proxy battle among shareholder activists and a Federal Trade Commission (FTC) investigation. His company weathered monopolistic accusations from the FTC and stalled merger attempts with their competitor. He was barred from blogging for 10 months until he was fully vindicated of wrongdoing by his board of directors and the Federal Trade Commission.

This social media experiment backfired and cost shareholders significant legal fees. Within a 12-month period, they witnessed a 50 percent stock price drop (Yahoo! Financial n.d.). Nobody can even guess how much brand erosion this created. Is it possible even for a company with an ostensibly high WQ to suffer from a poorly executed social media plan? Absolutely.

This story describes the woes of John Mackey, the CEO and chairman of Whole Foods Market. Even though their acquisition of Wild Oats Market finally closed in 2007, Mackey learned some emotionally taxing lessons. First, anything you say may be taken out of context, and can spread like a virus through all forms of digital media. Second, social media can test our good judgment. This digital drama reflects the magic—and the madness—of blindly embarking on a social media strategy (Kesmodel Wilke 2007).

Your *Energize*Growth® Plan is only as good as your ability to track your progress, effectively manage your brand, and honor your values. When you're in full control of that plan, and it is shared exclusively within the four walls of your company, life is good. When you have thrown your company's hat in the social media ring, things may change. Nothing shines a spotlight on your strengths and warts more than social media. Therefore, tracking your company's "word-of-mouse" activity and reaction is essential. These 11 guidelines should help you proceed with caution and avoid your own "Mackey Moment."

11 STEPS TO *ENERGIZE* YOUR SOCIAL MEDIA STRATEGY

1. *Proceed pragmatically.* Don't let social media fuel shiny penny syndrome. You may recall that story from Chapter 3. Prior to launching any social media program, ask yourself these questions:

- *How will this either help or hurt our company's (and my personal) purpose and vision?*

- *How will we feel if this content is pasted on the cover of the New York Times,* the *Economist,* or the *Wall Street Journal?*

- *Who will manage or maintain regular contact within the communities we have chosen to join?* You can create a lot of client discord and brand erosion by posting infrequent content, or abandoning the network altogether.

- *Where does my tribe (ideal clients, economic buyers, key influencers, and raving fans) spend their time?* Be sure your community will benefit from your contributions to the network before you invest time and energy. Find out where they congregate and go to them. Avoid forcing them to create yet another username and password. LinkedIn does an excellent job of defining their member demographic. On their web site, they boast a network of 27 million and growing. They are expanding by 1.3 million members per month. Over 750,000 of their members are senior executives with an average household income of $109,000 and average 41 years of age. In Nike's case, their Facebook tribe now exceeds 73,000 members. Seventh Generation launched a thriving community that eventually expanded to 75,000 followers in the latter half of 2008.

Unless you are in the entertainment, direct response (such as financial services or travel), or consumer goods industries, your market may not yet be ripe for what social media offers. Many advertising experts report that investing heavily in social media for B2B companies just does not make sense—yet. If you are targeting Americans between the ages of 15 and 34—which SRB Marketing estimates spend on average more than seven hours per week online (SRB Marketing 2008)—you may want to allocate some of your marketing dollars to the social media category.

2. *Carefully select your social media dream team.* As opposed to making some extra pocket change through affiliate sales or banner advertising, you can expand your influence and revenues faster by actively joining and strategically participating in select online groups.

Identify the company "ambassadors" who can speak on behalf of your company. Some team members may better represent your company's values than others due to seniority, communications skills, and insights into your strategic direction. Be sure those ambassadors are set up to succeed in that role—give them sufficient time to represent your company in a positive way, and be sure they respond quickly to community questions and concerns. They should have ample knowledge of your company to make thoughtful, valuable contributions.

If you use networks such as LinkedIn to post questions or recruit, seek out communities of like-minded individuals. Contribute to those groups. As time progresses, you will expand your footprint and brand message. If you find that certain networks are not attracting your ideal prospects or recruits, drop the membership. I have, for example, been asked to join tagged.com many times, and simply see no professional benefit. Every two weeks, I receive an annoying e-mail message that some acquaintance is "waiting for me on tagged."

You also may want to research Twitter, which is often referred to as a "micro blogging" tool. Others call it the next generation of instant messaging tools. When you join the Twitter community, you are prompted with the question, "What are you doing now?" A screen then allows you to enter up to 140 characters to respond. When people post messages, they are called "tweets." In the online retail category, Zappos CEO Tony Hsieh boasts over 300,000 devotees or followers.

Social networking expert Jason Alba recommends Twitter to develop close relationships with other authors and entrepreneurs, but reminds us that it doesn't happen overnight. He says:

> A lot of people tell me, "I don't care what you had for breakfast. I don't care if you're from Greece. I don't care what book you're reading." The interesting thing is, if you continue for weeks and months listening to people, learning about them and sharing some of the more intimate parts of your day or business, you really start to build a relationship with these people. (J. Alba, personal communication, May 20, 2008)

Social networking sites can help you find your "tribe" three different ways. First, they can help you locate contacts that are geographically close to you. Second, they help you find complementary product and service providers. I have found some highly talented authors and consultants who specialize in areas that I'm lacking, such as compensation, globalization, and recruiting. We routinely exchange ideas and review each other's blog postings. Finally, effective social networking sites can help you locate the power networkers. These people proudly post the number of connections they have, and have mastered the art of connecting people with relevant interests and values. On LinkedIn, power networkers usually boast over 500 professional connections. I have about 450 professionals in my network. They may be willing to help you recruit business partners or point you to a resource you need for a time-sensitive meeting or project.

3. *Study the user agreement before you join any social network.* There are some things on a personal profile that will cause you to get your hands slapped, such as putting your e-mail address in your name field. When you use LinkedIn, that's against the terms of service. Other networking sites have shut down users who leverage

the network as a perpetual online press release machine. One frequent LinkedIn user told me that he cringes every time he sees a question that is obviously designed to build traffic for their web site, request feedback on your recent blog post, or to announce a new product. Serious social networkers will spot you a mile away and run in the opposite direction. Facebook and LinkedIn have suspended many members for violating their terms—and it can often take several weeks to restore your service.

The best way to benefit from networking within your tribe is by helping other people. The more you help, the more that will come back to you. There's a lot to be said about the Law of Reciprocity, or the "give more than you get" principle. It is timeless.

4. *Know the intended outcome before you launch a social media strategy.* Do you simply want to increase your newsletter subscribers? Is it to expand your global reach? Do you want to be viewed as the go-to resource on retaining great employees or generating more sales? Social media may be a cost-effective vehicle to spread the word. David Wigder, author of *The Marketing Green Blog* and vice president of business development at RecycleBank, provides an interesting taxonomy of social networks. He identifies several different types or strategies. For example: (1) You may want to create an *interactive forum* where your clients can regularly post questions and concerns. This helps your online fans connect with each other offline (to purchase goods from one another, attend events together, form joint ventures, etc.). (2) You want to gather pledges, signatures, and commitments to a cause greater than your company. This is often called *cause marketing.* Seventh Generation and The Nature Conservancy do this very effectively. (3) You can design an *engagement site* to test out a new idea, share new ideas, and gather feedback. (4) Some social media outlets are purely designed as *shopping malls* (Wigder 2007). (5) Finally, you may want to simply use the media for *general information sharing.* This strategy is ideal for broadcasting special events and new offerings. If you are considered somewhat of

a celebrity or expert in your field, your raving fans want to know what you're doing, and whether you're coming to their town. Guy Kawasaki's blog does this brilliantly. Whenever he travels or attends an industry event, he posts photos and personal comments on the faces and places he has encountered.

Raymond Chip Lambert, president of Network2Networth LLC, has supplemented his direct selling efforts with LinkedIn. At the outset, he was very clear about what outcomes he expected from his media strategy. He wanted to become a leading source for business professionals who want to leverage their existing relationships through online social media. In 2008, Lambert generated $50,000 in new business using LinkedIn. That was just the beginning. As a result of his power networker status on LinkedIn, he recently launched a joint venture with a consulting firm that he expects will generate $8 million in new seminar and product sales within the next three years (R. Lambert, personal communication, May 20, 2008).

5. Develop a single, impressive, consistent company profile across a select few media sites. Jason Alba stresses that "developing your personal or company profile is the number one thing you need to do. If I find a profile with limited information in it, the message I get is, 'I don't care to network with you. I'm not here seriously. I'm still testing the waters.' "

Multiple social media interfaces introduce yet another complication. The different sites supposedly have interfaces that enable them to be connected, but in the short term no interoperability really exists. Further, there is no marketplace incentive for one site to help connect to another. Each site hopes to become the dominant site that everyone has to use, putting competitors out of business.

Markets take off only when consumers have a single and standard way of doing things. The social media market standard is still up for grabs. The PC revolution did not occur until multiple "not quite compatible" machines gave way to the IBM/Microsoft standard.

Individual companies, however, always seek a proprietary advantage—don't believe different, even in the age of open source.

Different industry segments have fought over database, e-mail, Web, and document formats. For nearly a decade, the HD-DVD and Blu-Ray formats competed for acceptance and market share for high-definition DVDs. Says author and business consultant Collins Hemingway, "Common sense said they would agree on a format so the industry could move ahead, but both hoped to win the arm-wrestling match. Blu-Ray finally did—after the high-def market had been paralyzed for years" (C. Hemingway, personal communication, October 5, 2008).

Today, the Blu-Ray disk format is supported by over 200 media, personal computer, and electronics manufacturers, but only after the market began to move away from DVDs to direct digital downloads (Blu-Ray 2008).

Until a true standard emerges, creating and managing multiple social or business networking sites will be frustrating and time consuming. This is a good enough reason to scare most of us away from expanding our social media footprint. As of this writing, we are forced to rely on our own "do-it-yourself" approaches to managing multiple company profiles and networks. We have not yet seen any clear leader in social media aggregation emerge.

Products from Atomkeep and Friendfeed, however, are making gains in this area. Unfortunately, setting up the connections to other sites is clumsy at best. Microsoft Live Mesh is an example of another approach entirely. It enables each person or company to set up a social site published online to anyone of your choosing. Instead of "pushing" your company data to a central site like Facebook, MySpace, or LinkedIn, such tools allow you to share files, blog posts, and relevant documents. This is called a peer-to-peer approach. As a result, you can better manage your brand because you are in charge of controlling all inbound and outbound traffic. This approach eliminates any copyright or privacy matters caused by one site taking content from another in the process of aggregation. The only information published is what you want published, and to whom you want it published.

I suggest taking a "wait-and-see" approach before you get too over-zealous about joining too many networks. Watch to see whether any particular aggregator becomes the dominant force in that category and gains overwhelmingly dominant share, or whether users create their own sophisticated webs of business and social contacts.

6. *Keep your current advertising relationships separate from your social media relationships.* In the future, I predict that social media firms will outnumber traditional public relations firms. I have yet to find any, traditional PR firms that have successfully launched a social media division. When I say successful, I mean they offer clients strategies for effectively leveraging, launching, and measuring the impact of select social media strategies. Even today, in an age where the client controls the remote, most agency sites open with fancy Flash video screens and direct me to electronic screen shots of the colorful client brochures they designed. When I recently scanned ad agency websites, I found that none could demonstrate their prowess at developing communities of raving fans or like-minded buyers. I doubt they have a clue about social media and "word-of-mouse" marketing. Instead, new game-changing firms such as Lotame, Appsserve, EchoDitto, Mindshare Interactive Campaigns, and SocialMedia will lead the way.

7. *Practice network netiquette.* Be respectful as you learn to use the network. Using these outlets to announce your new Web seminar, product suite, or team members is simply inappropriate. People want to be part of the conversation, not "sold to." Following complete strangers using Twitter is also a huge time waster and a distraction. Also, stay clear of following mass groups of people in these networks. Without discipline, these media outlets will try your patience and chew up lots of your time. They will fill your inbox faster than pleas from Nigerian con artists. Currently, companies like Twitter experience frequent outages due to network overload. If you rely too heavily

on one media outlet for your business development activity, you'll regret it.

Contribute to the networks by offering your expertise and insights. When you use LinkedIn, for example, regularly visit the "Answers" section. This is a great way to stay active on LinkedIn without having it take over your life. LinkedIn provides a "Subscribe to New Questions" feature that allows you to receive only the subject areas that interest you. You can find this feature on the "Profile Setup" page. For example, I subscribe to the business development and sustainability categories. This saves me a huge amount of time sorting through questions, and is an effective way to build my personal brand. You can also add the Answers postings to your Google Reader or Google Home page. This makes it very fast and easy to parse through relevant topics and questions.

8. *Never replace your high-value relationships with virtual ones.* You cannot protect yourself from public scrutiny, security breaches, or information leaks. And you will not create trusting relationships exclusively by joining an online group. Whether you use social media or pony express, you must continue to invest in building trusting relationships with your clients and community. Jim Cathcart, author of *Relationship Intelligence*, reminds us that:

> [A]lmost everything you achieve will be in some ways done through others. The more people you have helping you, the more likely you are to succeed. A high value relationship is one in which both participants receive substantial benefits. There are three essential characteristics of every high quality relationship:
>
> • Both parties are committed to the success of the relationship.
> • There must be enough trust for the truth to flow freely.
> • You need clear agreements. Both of you need to understand what to expect from the other person (Cathcart n.d.).

9. *Involve your sales and information technology groups in your social media strategy.* Lambert predicts that customer relationship management software firms (CRM companies) will launch a social component in future versions. They will offer tracking mechanisms and social analytics suites. For example, they will tell you how many connections your client has when they e-mail you. They may tell you what blogs they visit most frequently. Or what social networks they use. An early entrant in this market space is Xobni.com. This is an Outlook enhancer that can tell you who else is in your contact's social network. It also offers a LinkedIn plug-in tool. The time commitment required to stay abreast of this rapidly changing industry is significant. Leave this level of product research to the experts while you focus on setting your company direction and guiding your team.

10. *Be thyself.* If one of your company values is transparency, then act transparently. Do not create anonymous pen names in forums, blogs, or networks. Maintaining fresh content shows commitment. Be willing to admit to your organization's own shortcomings. When you respond to postings or questions, be sure not to sound terribly defensive. (When in doubt, return to Principle 1.) When you make a mistake, admit it. People will respect you for being human. These networks are designed primarily to engage and dialogue honestly with existing customers, strategic partners, and prospective customers. They are not designed to try to sell to them underhandedly or to defend your brand. Train your marketing team on ways to inform, educate, and inspire without blatantly promoting your products and services. If you want to sell something, then purchase advertising on those sites.

11. *Use social media to create positive change in the world.* These tools are a way to bring people together instead of tearing us asunder. Your clients, shareholders, and community need fresh ideas and inspiration. If you are a key executive within your company, it's your job to be an ambassador. Leave the nay-saying, personal attacks, and doomsday predictions out of your discussions. Visit LinkedIn and Google Answers and review some of the questions people are asking.

Then give away valuable information. I invest 30 minutes a week in helping people in these forums. I have developed great relationships with people as close by as Eugene, Oregon, and as far away as Dubai, United Arab Emirates.

When I graduated from college and got my first job in high technology sales in 1983, I could have never predicted how far the Information Age would evolve. We have an obligation to leverage this nascent medium in a positive way. By taking a strategic and cautious approach to social media, you will perpetuate trustworthy, high-value relationships. These quality relationships will create positive momentum with your *Energize* Growth® plan.

Energy Booster 11

How will we positively and strategically leverage social media to energize our growth plan?

Sample *Energize*Growth® Plan

Tydak Consulting Services, LLC

STRATEGIC MARKET IMPERATIVES

In most organizations, Information Technology (IT) departments are still perceived as cost centers and not strategic assets. Companies struggle to recognize the need to provide technology improvements in a proactive, strategic manner. This affects employee morale and can impact the company's competitive edge. IT must stay current with changes to systems, applications, processes, and procedures to stay competitive, avoid technology obsolescence, and, most importantly, be viewed as a trusted advisor by their company peers.

CFO Perspective

1. Cost to operate/support technology continues to rise.

2. No clear value of in-house IT identified.

3. End customer becomes unhappy with company's product or service.

4. Hesitant to authorize budget for technology expenses.

5. No confidence in the Chief Information Officer (CIO).

6. Unable to take advantage of technology to improve operating costs, reach new markets, increase productivity, deeper customer relationships, and so on.

7. Lack of key knowledge or business intelligence to promote better decisions and pursue new opportunities.

CIO Perspective

1. Potential to be fired or outsourced.

2. High turnover of best people increases within IT.

3. Low morale and low productivity.

4. Undervalued by business units.

5. Difficult to acquire budget for necessary technology expenses.

6. Constantly on the defensive.

7. Increase in number of failed projects.

Ultimate Result and Unique Value

1. *Solid ability to provide knowledge transfer to our clients*—our success is measured by their ability to look for continuous improvements in the value of IT.

2. Tydak's solutions include a tool to assist you in developing and maintaining *meaningful IT Metrics to ensure accountability and achievement of objectives.*

3. We don't just teach IT managers about service support and delivery; *we also teach business management.*

Ideal Client

1. The client's management team shares a common technology vision and is able to implement decisions to improve the company.

2. The company is striving to improve profit margins and is willing to be held accountable.

3. The company is under increased pressure to prove the value of technology. For example, CEOs are facing time-sensitive, external compliance guidelines including Sarbanes-Oxley, SEC regulations and other regulatory agencies. They may also be under great Board pressure to prove the value of IT.

4. IT Services are managed in-house.

5. The ideal sized IT shop is 8 to 100 persons.

6. Company is headquartered in the South/West region of the United States.

7. They can acquire budget to cover the initial costs of assessment and they require assistance to implement recommendations.

Elevator Statement

We help transform the relationships between business and Information Technology executives in Southern California by helping them to close the communication gap. We have consistently enabled our clients to recognize a 30 percent improvement in customer satisfaction and an immediate reduction in operating costs.

Three-Year Vision for Tydak

Tydak is recognized as a regional leader in business alignment with technology to gain measurable value.

Tydak's senior consultants participate in our clients' key information technology decisions.

Tydak is an industry leader in IT Performance Management in our region. Our IT metrics tool and process improvement techniques are invaluable to any IT organization that wants to serve the business community well and gain the respect of management.

Pat is a sought-after paid speaker on the subject of IT Alignment and Performance Management.

Our staff consists of 10 full-time employees including: Project Managers, Senior Consultants, Sales and Marketing team, and one Administrative Assistant. We maintain a network of 25 to 30 BI and ITSM consultants to meet the market demands. We continue to manage the business in a virtual office environment. Tydak employees continue to develop their skills and are challenged by the work.

Tydak's Values

Integrity—Say what you mean and mean what you say.

Timeliness—Deliver as promised, and be on time to meetings and appointments.

Willingness to Change—Recognize that staying the same will net the same results. When identifying a problem with the client, we do not place blame. Instead, we look for solutions and learn from past performance. We are open to new ideas. This applies to both Tydak and our clients.

Accountability—Accountable to clients for our deliverables and on all commitments. We expect the clients to be accountable as well. We expect them to take responsibility for the state of their department or project. This allows us to develop mutual trust—a cornerstone for our future success.

Leadership—We lead by example. We also assume others are bright, feeling and capable employees, and treat them as such.

Learning Environment—Our teams and strategic partners possess a strong desire to continue to grow through education and training. Clients should be of the same mindset for their staff and for themselves. . . . "You're never too old to learn."

Objectives for Growth

Critical Goal Category 1: We will strengthen our brand recognition within the IT Service Management and Business Intelligence market segments.

> *SMART Goal 1A:* Complete client interviews and case studies by March 1, 2009.

> *SMART Goal 1B:* Our senior consultants and executive staff will identify and attend at least two networking meetings per month by March 30, 2009.

> *SMART Goal 1C:* Revise company positioning document and upgrade brand touch points by July 1, 2009.

> *SMART Goal 1D:* Develop at least two new marketing action plans to generate new leads from new and existing clients (such as speaking, networking groups, search engine optimization, and social networking) by July 30, 2009.

Critical Goal Category 2: Develop a marketing plan for our IT Metrics product.

> *SMART Goal 2A:* Complete a C-level survey by January 31, 2009.

> *SMART Goal 2B:* Publish survey results on our web site and through trade association by June 30, 2009.

Critical Goal Category 3: Create a solid pipeline of qualified opportunities to achieve at least $5M in revenues by 2010.

SMART Goal 3A: Increase full time staff to five people by September 30, 2009.

What Gaps Are Keeping Tydak from Growth?

1. Lead Generation systems are not yet fully developed and automated.

2. Low public awareness.

3. Leadership is sometimes distracted by activities other than marketing (e.g., hiring, finance).

"Stop Doing" List

1. Stop allowing limiting beliefs to consume our schedules or activities (which lead to paralysis and procrastination).

2. Stop making excuses for avoiding networking meetings.

Measures of Success: *We are successful when . . .*

1. We are treated as a trusted advisor and consulted for staffing, software, or acquisition changes.

2. Our employees assume greater responsibility and feel a sense of pride and ownership in the organization and its growth.

3. We can easily predict each opportunity in the pipeline, and the flow of leads is distributed evenly across the various stages of our sales and marketing system.

4. Our sales cycle time from lead to client continues to shrink, and is predictable with 80 to 85 percent of leads.

5. Prospects ask us for assessments because of our reputation for developing accurate, achievable, clear, and concise recommendations.

6. Pat's monthly speaking schedule is steady and predictable.

APPENDIX B

Sample ProfitCents Report

Business Energy Boost - Performance Review

For

GREEN BUILDING ADVISORS INC.

For the period ending 09/30/2008

Provided By:

EnergizeGrowth

*Energize*Growth LLC
Lisa Nirell
541-593-8787

Disclaimer

10/24/2008

The information included in the following comparative financial evaluation is presented only for supplementary analysis and discussion purposes. Such information is presented for internal management use only and is not intended for third parties. Accordingly, we do not express an opinion or any other form of assurance on the supplementary information.

Green Building Advisors Inc.   Page 1

FIGURE B.1 ProfitCents Extreme Report Sample

Source: ProfitCents, Sageworks. Reprinted with permission.

Report prepared for: Green Building Advisors Inc.
Industry: Business Consultants
Revenue: $1M - $10M
Periods: 3 months against the 3 months that directly preceded them

SCORECARD		
★☆☆☆☆	LIQUIDITY
★★★★★	PROFITS & PROFIT MARGIN
★★★★★	SALES
★★★★★	BORROWING
★★★☆☆	ASSETS
★★★★★	EMPLOYEES

A NOTE ON SCORING: Each section of this report (Liquidity, Profits & Profit Margin, etc.) contains a star rating which measures the company's overall performance in the area at the time of the report's generation. One star indicates that the company is below average or may possibly need improvement in the area. Three stars indicate that the company is about average for the area. Five stars indicate that the company is above average or performing quite well in the area.

LIQUIDITY

Generally, what is the company's ability to meet obligations as they come due?

Operating Cash Flow Results
The company has generated negative cash flow from operations, yet the company is profitable. This is somewhat unusual and may reflect a problem, since overall liquidity conditions on the Balance Sheet are soft/weak, which will be discussed below. Given overall conditions, it seems like the company may have some difficulty in this area for the period. If profits reflect real economic progress, it seems like working capital accounts may need to be more effectively managed.

General Liquidity Conditions
It is positive that the company's liquidity numbers are looking better than they did last period, but considerably more improvement may still be needed. Basically, **the liquidity position is still quite poor**. Both the current ratio and the quick ratio are weak as depicted in the graph area of the report. This assessment is made by a careful evaluation of the firm's data AND the data of other similar companies in the industry. These ratios are benchmarks for the business, which indicate that both the scope (size) and composition (quality) of the company's liquidity base are poor.

The firm needs to improve conditions in this area -- it must **continue** to do better on the Income Statement side by driving in more profits AND by finding ways to retain the additional cash flow in the company. Otherwise, the firm could **possibly** have some difficulties paying bills over the long run.

This period, although the company may need to improve some components of liquidity, it is doing average work with regard to inventory days, accounts receivable days, and accounts payable days. Nothing drastic needs to occur here with these metrics. If the company needs more cash specifically, it may want to drop its AR days ratio over time, which reflects the firm's ability to collect receivables and get cash.

Tips For Improvement
Here are some possible actions that management might consider if appropriate (these are ideas that might be thought about):

- Complete projects on a timely basis. If completion takes longer than expected, soft costs such as interest and penalties can start to drain the money coming into the business.
- Set longer terms for Accounts Payable when possible. For example, increase a 30 day payment window to 60 days.
- Sell any unnecessary/unproductive assets the business may have to increase cash. These are assets that are not contributing sufficiently to the generation of income and cash flow.

- Increase prices selectively where possible. Done effectively, this can boost cash flow and liquidity. Good Income Statement management helps Balance Sheet performance.

LIMITS TO LIQUIDITY ANALYSIS: Keep in mind that liquidity conditions are volatile and this is a general analysis looking at a snapshot in time. Review this section, but do not overly rely on it.

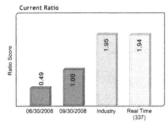

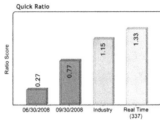

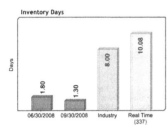

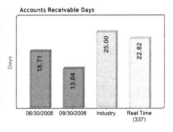

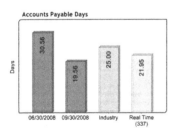

PROFITS & PROFIT MARGIN

Are profitability trends favorable in the company?

Results this period are up from last period. The company is performing quite well here -- better than most other firms in this industry. In fact, the company has received the highest score possible in this area. First, **net profitability is strong**. This means that the company is earning higher net profits than most of its competitors, as determined by the industry and sales range that the company operates in. It also means that net profits have increased substantially from last period. If the company can continue to generate better net profits over time, it is likely to improve performance in all other areas of the report as well. Net profit margins are also high, which indicates general profit health.

Second, both gross profit margins and net profit margins have improved from last period, which is excellent. This means that the company is managing direct costs (cost of sales) and indirect costs (general and administrative costs) very effectively. Trends are very important in this area. It is good to see that the company is becoming more efficient over time.

Third, it is good to increase sales this much and control expenses this well concurrently. Sales results are typically only important in so much as they affect profitability. These results indicate that the company is managing its growth well. It may also mean that the company should think of how to lever higher profits in the future. The time to grow the business is **when profitability and liquidity are strong.**

Tips For Improvement
The following ideas to improve profitability might be useful and can be thought-through by managers:

- Diversify the business offerings so that if one area hits a dry patch, solid profitability can still be earned. For example, consider offering consultation services for residential and commercial remodeling projects.
- Plan for potential problems before you start the job. This will help you reduce the post-job client punchlist, which costs you extra time and money.
- Establish uniqueness in the product or service the business offers -- a unique selling feature. By doing so, the business can generate increased demand for its offering and potentially increase prices as well.
- Obtain an annual business check-up. Meet with an accountant or banker to review financial statements and get advice on how to improve performance.

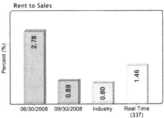

SALES

★★★★★

Are sales growing and satisfactory?

Significant increases in sales occurred this period. In fact, sales are even growing at a faster rate than the sales of many competitors, a positive result. This dynamic should help to improve profitability over time if other Income Statement accounts are being managed well. The organization has also added some fixed assets, but sales have increased at a higher rate than the rate at which the asset base has increased, which is another key trend. This means that assets are generating more sales than they were last period. Still, the firm's overall focus should remain **on managing profitability, not sales**. This section of the report is generally less important than the Liquidity or Profitability sections.

BORROWING

★★★★★

Is the company borrowing profitably?

Net profitability improved by 222.66% while debt was lowered. In other words, a reduction in total debt coincided with improved profitability, at least for this period. Not only this, but the net profit margins and overall liquidity actually improved. This is a very good situation -- profitability was able to expand without additional debt. This dynamic should help long-term profitability, especially if it can be continued over multiple periods.

There are a few other notes. The overall score in this area is quite good. The company does not have substantial amounts of debt on its Balance Sheet when compared with other companies in the industry. Also, it seems to be generating "average" earnings (before interest and non-cash expenses) compared to its interest obligations. Since debt is used less than in other similar companies, it could be that debt is generally less important to overall conditions. Additional exploration of this issue by managers would be necessary for further conclusions.

Capacity planning is a challenge here. This involves simply thinking out into the future: how long can profitability improve without increasing borrowing? Analyzing the relationship between investments in resources (such as assets) and profitability improvement, as well as effectively forecasting sales and cash flow, can help answer this question and lead to the best borrowing policies for the near future.

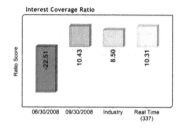 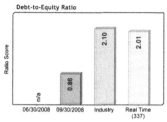

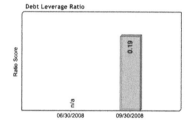

ASSETS

Is the company using gross fixed assets effectively?

The company performed well here. There were additions to fixed assets and profitability improved by even more. If profitability can consistently improve more quickly than assets, the company should see a strong long-run return on assets. It is unusual and positive that net margins and overall liquidity have improved as the company has added assets. Yet increasing assets further could be problematic because the rise in net profitability and overall liquidity compared with the increase in assets could be coincidental, not bearing any significant relationship.

The company seems to be doing an average job with its assets. However, it generated relatively poor returns on its assets and equity this period, which may be of some concern. On a positive note, the company appears to be producing strong sales from its fixed asset base. Over time, if sustained, this could help improve their returns on assets and equity.

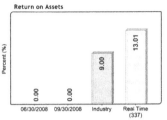

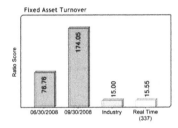

EMPLOYEES

Is the company hiring effectively?

Net profitability improved significantly this period, even though the employee base stayed fairly flat. This is very positive because it means that the company is **improving its net profitability per employee statistic**. Improving this statistic is important because it means that the company is managing its employee base more efficiently.

As discussed earlier in the Assets section of the report, the company's fixed assets have increased as well. It is always important to evaluate the source of net profitability -- what resources caused this profitability improvement? Right now, managers **might** be somewhat reluctant to hire more people because the company has improved profitability with a relatively level employee base. Employees cost money, so if the company can improve profitability without adding more people, it will often choose not to hire. On the other hand, if the company has "maximized" employee efficiency, managers will need to hire more people in the future to continue increasing profitability. Hiring decisions should be planned carefully in this company.

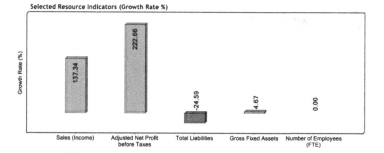

References

Allegiance. n.d. Employee voice. www.allegiance.com/employeevoice/ index.php (accessed October 23, 2008).

Bedbury, S. 2001. All aboard the brandwagon. In *A new brand world*, 11. New York: Viking Penguin. Used by permission of Viking Penguin, a division of Penguin Group (USA) Inc.

Blu-Ray. n.d. About. www.blu-ray.com/info/ (accessed October 23, 2008).

Cathcart, J. 2000. *Relationship intelligence.* e-book. www.cathcart.com.

Cerius Interim Executive Solutions. 2008. *Risky business: Five big risks that can kill your business.* Alison Viejo, CA: Cerius Interim Executive Solutions.

Collins, J. 2001. *Good to great: Why some companies make the leap and others don't.* New York: HarperCollins.

Consumers await on social networks. 2008, October 10. www.emarketer. com/Article.aspx?id=1006622 (accessed October 23, 2008).

Covey, S. R. 2004. *The 8th habit: From effectiveness to greatness.* New York: Simon & Schuster.

Davis, R., with A. Shrader. 2007. *Leading for growth: How Umpqua Bank got cool and created a culture of greatness.* San Francisco: Jossey-Bass.

Drucker, P. F., with J. A. Maciariello. 2004. *The daily Drucker: 366 days of insight and motivation for getting the right things done.* New York: HarperCollins.

Dweck, C. S. 2006. *Mindset: The new psychology of success.* New York: Random House.

Frankl, V. E. 1992. *Man's search for meaning: An introduction to logotherapy.* Boston: Beacon Press. Used with permission.

Gerber, M. 1995. *The e-myth revisited: Why most small businesses don't work and what to do about it.* New York: HarperCollins.

Giovagnoli, M. 2008, January 14. Networlding: The science of networking. *The Connections Show* (podcast 017). http://connections.thepodcastnetwork.com/2008/01/14/connections-017-networlding-the-science-of-networking/ (accessed October 23, 2008).

Google Finance, s.v. NASDAQ:UMPQ, http://finance.google.com/finance?q=NASDAQ:UMPQ (accessed October 23, 2008).

Gyatso, T. (the fourteenth Dalai Lama). 2008, October 21. Compassion and the individual. http://dalailama.com/page.166.htm.

Hart, C. W. L. 1988. The power of unconditional service guarantees. *Harvard Business Review*, July–August, 88405: 59.

Hay Group. 2007. Dangerous liaisons, mergers, and acquisitions: The integration game (White paper available on request from the Hay Group, www.haygroup.com).

Holtzman, S. 2007. Key focused questions to keep companies healthy: An interview with JELD-WEN and EnergizeGrowth. *Cascade Business News* 14 (17): 57.

Howard, C. 2004. *Turning passions into profits: 3 steps to wealth and power.* Hoboken, NJ: John Wiley & Sons.

Jeld-Wen Communities. Our philosophy. www.jeld-wencommunities.com/Our-Philosophy.html (accessed October 23, 2008).

Katie, B. 2008. The work of Byron Katie. www.thework.com (accessed November 4, 2008).

Kawasaki, G. 2004. *The art of the start: The time-tested, battle-hardened guide for anyone starting anything.* New York: Penguin Books.

Keiningham, T. L., L. Aksoy, A. B. Cooil, et al. 2008. Linking customer loyalty to growth. *MIT Sloan Management Review* 49 (4): 2.

Kesmodel, D., and J. R. Wilke. 2007. Whole Foods is hot—Wild Oats a dud: So said "Rahodeb"; Then again, Yahoo poster was a Whole Foods staffer, the CEO to be precise. *Wall Street Journal*, July 12. http://online.wsj.com/article/SB118418782959963745.html (accessed October 22, 2008).

Kotter, J. P., and J. L. Heskett. 1992. *Corporate culture and performance.* New York: Simon & Schuster.

Lay, P. 2006. The four D's: Critical segmentation criteria for targeting SMBs (E-mail viewletter). *Under the Buzz: Commentary on Business Strategy Issues for Executives in Enterprise Systems & Software Companies* 7 (1).

Maister, D. H. 1997. *True professionalism: The courage to care about your people, your clients, and your career.* New York: Simon & Schuster.

McLaughlin, M. 2004, November 28. Pricing redux: How to dump hourly rates. http://guerrillaconsulting.typepad.com/guerrilla_marketing_for _c/2004/11/pricing_redux_h.html (accessed October 23, 2008).

Middleton, R. 2008. *Fast track to more clients, marketing workbook: 7 simple steps to attracting more clients.* Boulder Creek, CA: Action Plan Marketing.

Minor, N. 2003. *Deciding to sell your business: The key to wealth and freedom.* Denver, CO: Minor & Brown.

Pausch, R. 2008, April 9. The last lecture: A love story for your life, Part 1. Interview by Diane Sawyer, ABC News Program.

Radcliffe Public Policy Center. 2002. Life's work: Attitudes toward work and life integration, 2000. Murray Research Archive [Distributor]. hdl:1902.1/00021/.

Shirlaws Coaching. 2005. *Stages of development: Shirlaws coaching model.* Sydney, Australia: Shirlaws Coaching.

Sipe, M. 2008. *Cashing out: How to prepare, position and sell your company for top dollar* (Special Report). San Diego, CA: Crosspointe Capital.

SRB Marketing. 2008. *Green social networks: A special report.* New Paltz, NY: SRB Marketing.

Stein, M. 2003. *How to develop the perfect elevator pitch.* Vistage International. http://www.vistage.com/featured/how-to-develop-the-perfect-elevator-speech.html.

Tom's of Maine. n.d. Charter documents. www.tomsofmaine.com (accessed October 23, 2008).

Twist, L., with T. Barker. 2003. *The soul of money: Reclaiming the wealth of our inner resources.* New York: W.W. Norton. www.soulofmoney.org.

Vieira, J. 2007. Discovery: Reading people and buyer types; the 8 Different ATB (Approach to Business) Types. The QMP Group.

Weiss, A. 2002. *Value-Based Fees: How to charge—and get—what you're worth: Powerful techniques for the successful practitioner.* San Francisco: Jossey-Bass/Pfeiffer.

Weiss, A. 2003. *Million Dollar Consulting: The professional's guide to growing a practice.* New York: McGraw-Hill.

Weiss, A. 2006, October 16. Alan Weiss said. http://davidmaister.com/blog/230/Value-Pricing (accessed October 23, 2008).

Weiss, A. 2007. The Million Dollar Consulting College®. www.summitconsulting.com.

Wigder, D. 2007, December 1. Green marketing on social networks. http://marketinggreen.wordpress.com/2007/12/01/green-marketing-on-social-networks/ (accessed October 23, 2008).

Wikipedia, s.v. "disruptive technology," http://en.wikipedia.org/wiki/Disruptive_technology, (accessed September 19, 2008).

Yahoo! Finance, s.v. Whole Foods Market Inc. (WFMI), http://finance.yahoo.com/q/hp?s=WFMI&a=00&b=1&c=2007&d=07&e=31&f=2008&g=m/ (accessed October 23, 2008).

YPartnership. 2007. Annual travel survey of 2,100 leisure travelers in the United States. *National Travel Monitor.*

About the Author

Lisa is the Chief Energy Officer of *Energize* Growth® (www. energizegrowth.com) in Bend, Oregon. She and her team help growth companies that aspire to increase profitability, attract great clients, and reach their company's full value potential.

As a strategic growth and marketing expert, Lisa has worked with hundreds of entrepreneurs, as well as Sony, Microsoft, Oppen-heimerFunds, Oracle, and BMC Software. Within just two years, she helped her clients generate $84 million in new business. Lisa is a sought-after speaker for entrepreneur groups and trade associations around the globe.

Lisa stays energized by hiking the great outdoors with her husband, Magnus, open water swimming, and yoga.

To download your bonus planning guides and tools, visit www.energizegrowth.com/egnow.shtml.

Index

Printed in the United States
By Bookmasters